QUESTIONING AND TEACHING:
A MANUAL OF PRACTICE

Questioning and Teaching

A MANUAL OF PRACTICE

J.T. DILLON

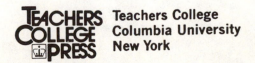

Teachers College
Columbia University
New York

© 1988 J.T. Dillon
Croom Helm Ltd, Provident House,
Burrell Row, Beckenham, Kent BR3 1AT
Croom Helm Australia, 44–50 Waterloo Road,
North Ryde, 2113, New South Wales

Published in the USA by
Teachers College Press
1234 Amsterdam Ave.
New York, NY 10027

Library of Congress Cataloging-in-Publication Data

Dillon, J. T.
   Questioning and teaching.

   Includes index.
   1. Questioning. 2. Teaching. I. Title.
LB1027.44.D55 1988   371.3′7   88-2216

ISBN 0-8077-2924-8 (pbk.)

Filmset by Mayhew Typesetting, Bristol, England

96 95 94 93 92 91 90 89   9 8 7 6 5 4 3 2

To the Socrates within us

Contents

List of Figures viii
Foreword ix

1 The Practice of Questioning 1

2 Student Questions 6
    The Place of Student Questions 8
    The Process of Questioning 17
    The Pedagogy of Student Questions 23
    Correlated Readings 34
    Practical Exercises 36

3 Teacher Questions 42
    Uses of Teacher Questions 46
    Questioning to Purpose 53
    Pedagogy of Teacher Questions 62
    Correlated Readings 75
    Practical Exercises 77

4 Questioning and Recitation 84
    Characteristics of Recitation 86
    Use of Questions and Answers 97
    An Alternative Recitation 103
    Correlated Readings 110
    Practical Exercises 112

5 Questioning and Discussion 116
    Characteristics of Discussion 120
    Use of Questions 127
    Use of Alternatives 132
    Using Questions and Alternatives 167
    Correlated Readings 171
    Practical Exercises 173

Appendix: Classroom Transcripts 176
Subject Index 194

Figures

Figure 2.1 The Process of Questioning   19
Figure 2.2 Pedagogy of Student Questions   24
Figure 3.1 Questioning to Purpose   54
Figure 3.2 Pedagogy of Teacher Questions   64
Figure 4.1 Pedagogy of Recitation Questions   99
Figure 5.1 Pedagogy of Discussion Questions   128
Figure 5.2 Alternatives to Questioning   133

Foreword

Teacher education has a long tradition of concern for the skills teachers need if they are to ask good questions. Learning, it is assumed, is an outgrowth of the questions that students are asked and the better a teacher's questions, the better a teacher's teaching and a class's learning. To know how to question is to know how to teach — or so it is assumed.

In a review-essay published in 1982 entitled 'The effect of questions in education and other enterprises' James Dillon showed that in fields like counselling and personal interviewing, fields that seek to encourage both talking and thinking on the part of their clients, practitioners are urged to avoid questions. On the other hand, in fields like courtroom advocacy and public opinion surveying questions are encouraged, and practitioners are highly skilled in putting questions — but the self-conscious goal in such fields is to limit the thoughtfulness, and to control the utterances, of the people being questioned. Professor Dillon pointed out that, of the fields he examined in preparing that essay, only education seemed to believe that asking questions of 'clients' would stimulate thoughtfulness and encourage expression.

This essay encouraged us to invite Professor Dillon to think about extending the ideas he raised there and to prepare a book on teaching. We believe that our enthusiasm about the line of thought that he opened up for us has been amply justified. *Questioning and Teaching* starts by making the case for seeing education as being an activity which is similar to, and not different from, such other fields. The opening chapters show that, just as in trial advocacy and public opinion surveys, questioning by teachers is an exercise of power and control — and thus limits authentic discussion and discourages questioning by students. But, and this is the core of everything that follows, questioning by students and the discussion which follows, can be regarded as the starting point for effective education, just as it is the starting point for effective counselling. As he writes elsewhere, 'No other event better portends learning than a question arising in the mind.' Questions invite a search for answers and the further questions which follow from answers, and if it is this kind of search that schools are seeking to encourage, it is pupils' questioning and questions, and the answers given their questions by students, that teachers should be encouraging and supporting. No other task is more important for both curriculum research and teacher education than that of showing what the consequences of this insight might be.

Showing teachers that they might design lessons which encourage students' questions and answers is the purpose of this book. Professor Dillon draws on his observations of classrooms, on educational, psychological and philosophical research, and on his own practice to offer a handbook of ideas for teachers who want to encourage thinking by students. His approach is practical in that he describes techniques that teachers might use in their classrooms as well as experiences that they might apply to enhance their understanding of the dynamics of a learning that is based on authentic and open-ended questioning by their students. As such this book pursues a theme that one of the earlier books in this series, Herbert Thelen's *The Classroom Society* (Croom Helm and John Wiley and Sons, 1981) sought to explore, and it is a basic theme which undergirds so much of contemporary educational thought: how can we make classrooms places in which true and meaningful learning on the part of all students is the norm?

This book is significant for the themes it develops but it is also important for the ways in which it works out its ideas and presents them to teachers. As we know all too well, education is replete with 'theory' that seems to have no application to the classroom and 'practical' manuals that have no clear starting point in a vision of what the classroom might be. *Questioning and Teaching* self-consciously brings these too often disparate strands of thinking together in what might be thought of as a new kind of model for both texts and courses in teacher education — rich in 'theory' but at the same time firmly practical in their concerns.

We are in a period in which teacher education is experiencing renewed interest on both sides of the Atlantic and the Pacific oceans; new models for teacher education are being proposed and new structures are being put in place to support the education of teachers — but many of us are concerned that the necessary interest in institution-building is running far, far ahead of curriculum development in this vital field. *Questioning and Teaching* will have an important role to play in what we assume must be the next stage of concern with the tasks of teacher education. It serves as a model for a new kind of course in teacher education that has the promise of both developing teacher skills and understandings and improving practice in fundamental ways. In short, we are convinced that this is an important book and we welcome it to the Croom Helm series on Curriculum Policy and Research.

W.A. Reid
University of Birmingham, England

Ian Westbury
University of Illinois at
Urbana/Champaign, USA

1

The Practice of Questioning

Ever since the time that Socrates first exemplified their use, questions have seemed promising devices for the pursuit of right knowing and acting. Scientists and scholars, among others, pose questions in systematic search of grounded knowledge. Educators too, especially in recent years, have taken to the systematic use of questions for teaching and learning. That is the practice of questioning at issue in this book. How are questions rightly used to serve educative purposes?

Education is a moral enterprise, inducing the young into the good. Schooling is one agency of education, teaching one process, and the classroom one place. Questioning is one device to serve educative purposes in classroom circumstances. This book is a manual for teachers on the practice of questioning. Although rendered for classroom teaching, its themes might also inform practice in other places, processes, and agencies within the grand enterprise of education.

In classroom circumstances, the practice of questioning describes the use of student and teacher questions during recitation and discussion. These four topics of practice form four chapters of the book: student questions, teacher questions, questioning in recitation, and questioning in discussion.

Each topic is treated comprehensively in its own right, as well as in relation to the other three topics. For instance, student questions are treated in relation to teacher questions, and teacher questions in relation to recitation and discussion questions; while recitation and discussion are treated as both student and teacher questioning. In that way each successive chapter anticipates subsequent ones and reflects previous ones.

The heart of the matter is found in every chapter. The themes of practice are fully displayed over the topic at hand, with allusions to the other topics as these enter into play with the featured topic. These related points surface briefly in any one chapter and in turn figure extensively as features of another chapter. The same themes of practice recur throughout, with variations around the topic of each chapter.

In rendering these themes each chapter moves through the same general format. The chapter begins with a summary or overview, proceeds through a narrative text illustrated with actual classroom exchanges, and ends in activities for study and practice of the chapter's themes. Details of this general format will enhance the reader's initial sense of the book, and may be used to guide reading and other systematic uses of it.

Each chapter features a half-dozen summary devices. The *chapter outline* appears on the first, facing page. Beyond an initial view of the chapter's content and structure, the outline serves as a detailed guide to study and review, as well as for doing some of the exercises at chapter's end. For example, one exercise is to practise formulating questions by making a question-outline of the chapter.

The first page of text begins with a paragraph of *introduction*, next a few paragraphs giving a general *summary* of the chapter, followed by a paragraph of *overview* for the chapter's main sections. These plus the final paragraphs in *conclusion* at end of text can be perused for the four chapters in succession, as a way of gathering the themes of the book. The initial paragraphs can also usefully be read again at chapter's end, as a way of emerging from the detail and recovering the themes of the text.

Further summary devices appear in chapter's midst. A *boxed scheme* summarises in outline form the pedagogy of questions for that chapter's topic; for example, the pedagogy of student questions, the pedagogy of recitation questions. The four boxes in the book may be examined together to see at a glance the interrelated scheme of action for the teacher's use of student and teacher questions during recitation and discussion. *Figures* and *tables* also summarise selected points in the text. They serve for perusal of the book, guide to close reading, device for study and review, and further for doing some of the exercises at chapter's end.

Apart from these summary devices, the body of the chapter is a narrative text illustrated with classroom exchanges. The narrative is devoted to the practice of questioning. That means it is not, among other things, a narrative of research reporting empirical studies, issues, and findings about classroom questioning. These can be found in the readings at end of chapter. The text of the chapter proceeds over practice, describing useful aspects of questions as devices for teaching.

The *narrative* develops in the same way through all four chapters. First it describes the characteristics of questions in classroom practice; for example, the characteristics of questions in recitation, and in discussion. Then it identifies the elements of questioning that are involved in conditions of practice; for example, the process that a student goes through in asking a question in class. Finally the text proposes a pedagogy of questions, or a scheme of teacher action for using questions; for example, the pedagogy of student questions, and of teacher questions. The pedagogy is simple, entailing one disciplined action before, during, and after asking the question — as outlined in the boxed scheme displayed in chapter's midst.

Illustrations and *examples* appear at every point in the text, drawn from actual classrooms observed and transcribed by the author. In addition to the dozens of point-for-point examples, each chapter begins with a more extensive set of classroom exchanges; for instance, excerpts from a characteristic recitation, a characteristic discussion. Still more extensive illustrations are the six transcripts of recitations and discussions found in the *Appendix*. These can be used to see all the chapter's points working at once, as it were; and they serve for doing some of the exercises at chapter's end. Although the illustrations are drawn from secondary classrooms (ages 16–18), the points that they illustrate knowingly apply to all levels — specifically to pre-school, primary, secondary, and tertiary. These illustrative exchanges are merely examples, instances of the general point. Matters that do not apply to classroom teaching at all levels are deliberately excluded from the book.

At the point where the narrative ends, the chapter continues with lists of related readings and exercises. These complete the work of the chapter through activities of study and practice over the chapter's themes.

Correlated Readings are selected sources for further study. They number about 100 items in all, two dozen per chapter, half from education and half from other fields concerned with questioning. Each source is selected for its merit in relation to some point in the chapter. A short note for each item indicates its general content or interest.

The readings are correlated with the text and also with one another. They supplement or elaborate the points made with fresh material and with other perspectives. Here, for instance, are the research studies giving a kind of narrative not found in the chapter. The readings from other fields deal with the chapter's themes in ways not found in education sources. For instance, they supply theories of questioning and models of question-answer relations, or they describe other contexts and techniques of practice. Together the readings develop the themes of the chapter from all possible angles through theoretical, empirical, and practitioner literature from two dozen fields that have something to contribute on these points. An individual reader can pursue any point of interest through one source from education plus one from another field. Various students might each select an interesting source to study and to report on for class discussion and mutual benefit. Correlated with the text of the chapter, the readings form a complementary program for learning about questions and their good use in classroom practice.

Practical Exercises are not for study but for action. They are activities for practising selected points of the chapter. Together the forty exercises, ten per chapter, form a complementary program for acting out the points that have been read in the text and perhaps studied further in the readings. The result is a comprehensive understanding of questions, and a practical one.

The exercises are designed for multiple uses. Any one can be selected with benefit, or several can be followed in a series. For instance, the ten exercises on teacher questions interrelate in a cumulative way. The exercises can be done as an individual, as a team or group, or yet as a whole-class activity. Moreover, each student may first do the exercise as an individual, then join with other students to report and to discuss their various findings; or several students may each do a different part of the same exercise and then combine their results. Finally, the exercises may be done *before* reading the chapter as well as after. By doing a practical exercise beforehand, the student will garner pertinent experience raising pointed questions to bring to the reading of the chapter and to the class activity over it.

Thus equipped with summary devices, narrative text, classroom illustrations, correlated readings, and practical exercises, the book lends itself to a variety of systematic uses in whole and in part. Taken together, the four chapters and the components of each chapter form a comprehensive program of instruction on the practice of questioning. Each chapter offers a complete program on its topic, and each component offers a complementary program. The narrative is a program of reading, the readings a program of correlated study, and the exercises a program of related action. All three programs can be followed throughout the four chapters; or one and another program may be selected for one or all chapters. For use as a course text, the book disposes material suitable for class lecture and discussion, for student study assignments and 'clinical' practice, and for review and examination. The material is arranged for easy selection of topics and selective combination of components without any loss of the themes of practice.

There is no mystery to the good use of questions while teaching. Everything in this book is well within the reach of the willing teacher. The better thing to reach for is not technique but understanding — an understanding of the elements of questioning so that with effort of thought and discipline of action we can bend them to the purposes and circumstances of our teaching. That is a practical understanding, the kind that informs practice.

To inform our practice, this book proposes an understanding of student and teacher questions during recitation and discussion. It offers to you my best practical answer to the question, 'How are questions rightly used to serve educative purposes?' You too will answer this question in your practice of questioning.

2

Student Questions

OVERVIEW

THE PLACE OF STUDENT QUESTIONS
Eleven Student Questions
Constraints of Discourse
   Cycles of interaction
   Rules of talk
   Norms of behavior

THE PROCESS OF QUESTIONING
Perplexity
Asking
Answering
Learning

THE PEDAGOGY OF STUDENT QUESTIONS
Provide for student questions
   Make room for them
   Invite them in
   Wait patiently for them
Welcome the question
Sustain the asking

CORRELATED READINGS

PRACTICAL EXERCISES

Figure 2.1: The process of questioning
Figure 2.2: Pedagogy of student questions

6

Student Questions

Whose question? determines the issue of teaching and learning. Just as asking precedes answering in the questioning process, so do student questions come before teacher questions in the learning process. For when students ask, learning follows in answer.

'These, then, are the kinds of question we ask,' proposed Aristotle, 'and it is in the answers to these questions that our knowledge consists' (*Posterior Analytics*, 89b). The questions arise in ignorance and perplexity, stimulating the student's thought and empowering his action in an energetic pursuit of inquiry coming to term in an answer. Question and answer conjoin to form knowledge and understanding. The student's knowledge consists in the proposition that he forms of question plus answer; his understanding inheres in the relation he construes between question and answer. These as possessions of the student are learning. In that way, student questions eventuate in learning.

That is all there is to it. If we understand as much, we need to know no more about student questions. But we still have much to do about them. For, as a rule, students do not ask questions. There is little room for their questions in normal practice, and little rhyme or reason for them to ask. They are busied with other things, notably giving answers to teacher questions. Classroom discourse normatively proceeds in ways that rule out student questions, while other powerful conditions and facts of life give students good reason not to ask. With most odds against the asking, students understandably ask few questions.

The willing teacher can do little enough against these odds to ensure that students will ask questions in class. The first pedagogical act is to understand. Practice follows, inspired by an appreciative and informative understanding of student questions — their service to learning and teaching, their place in the classroom, the conditions under which they emerge or hide, the process they follow from initial perplexity through to eventual learning.

Informed by our understanding, practice moves us to take action before, during, and after a student asks a question. First we provide for student questions, making systematic room for them in our classroom, inviting them in, and awaiting them patiently. Next we welcome them when they come, listening and attending to them as they are being asked. Then we sustain the student and the question in the asking. That is to discipline pedagogical behavior in service of educative purpose in classroom circumstance.

In order to inform our practice, here we will first examine the *place of student questions*, in actual classroom practice. Next we conceive the *process of questioning*, picturing it to ourselves from start to finish. Then we consider the *pedagogy of student questions*, those disciplined acts that a willing teacher can take to open a suitable place for the process of student questions to arise and for learning to follow in answer.

THE PLACE OF STUDENT QUESTIONS

Student questions enjoy generous place in educational theory but small room in classroom practice. Although learning follows in answer to a student question, few student questions are asked and even fewer are answered — at least aloud in classrooms. This oddity turns out to be perfectly understandable. Once we understand it appreciatively, we can find ways to open a suitable place for student questions in our classroom.

Eleven student questions

To illustrate the oddity of student questions in normal classroom practice, we will examine the case of the eleven student questions.

Let us visit some classrooms where discussions are going on — not lectures, seatwork, and so forth. Discussion classes are a sensible place to look for student questions, especially in social studies discussions in upper secondary classrooms (ages 16–18). We go into six schools and 27 classrooms, staying the full hour but scrutinising a ten-minute period, chosen at random, for each room. Amidst all of this we find eleven student questions.

Here they are, these Eleven, along with the topic under discussion in that class. These are the matters that the students are inquiring about.

Abortion

1. Were there more pregnancies in, like the 1940s and '50s than there are now?

American Revolution

2. When did the draft come about?
3. Who'd pay for it — Congress itself?

Environmental pollution

4. Is there any way they can check the water for that, you know, before you —?
5. Couldn't they possibly seal [pollutant containers], or is it too messy?
6. Does it come out in a powder, or —?

A racist trial

7. Y'all got into the courtroom yesterday?
8. Was that his wife?
9. And was that lady there, who hit his car?

Smoking

10. I was just wondering, like — I dunno, this might be kinda dumb and stuff — but OK, like you said, 'What is the Christian attitude to people who smoke?' So, does that mean if you smoke, you're not a Christian?

Marriage

11. Yeah, I want to ask you a question. What country do they have this, like when girls are young and boys are real young, you know, the parents, they already know that they're going to marry?

Let us work out the frequencies. First, we have visited 27 classrooms and heard eleven student questions. That is not one question per classroom, nor one every other classroom. We have had to visit three classrooms in a row to hear a single question from students.

Second, we have seen 721 students engaging in discussion and we have heard questions from eight of them. No questions from the other 99 per cent. Not a single question from 713 adolescents nearing graduation from secondary school.

Third, we have heard a lot of questions from the teachers. Questions accounted for over 60 per cent of the teachers' talk and for less than one per cent of the students' talk. The overall rate works out to 80 questions per hour from each teacher and two questions per hour from all the students combined.

All of that is normal practice, found everywhere. We may think that we have chanced on a bad day in every single one of the 27

9

classrooms. Or perhaps we visited six really bad schools, or the wrong level of schooling to begin with. Our thinking is wishful, for the known facts of the matter are against us. No one has ever walked into a sample of classrooms in any school at any level and heard a lot of student questions. To the very contrary. You can go and see for yourself. Children may well ask a lot of questions, but not in school. And the older they get, the fewer questions they ask. By the time of advanced graduate study, students have answered thousands upon thousands of questions, only to have a time of it thinking up a single question to ask for their thesis or dissertation research.

The Eleven are questions in search of *information, knowledge* and *understanding* about the subject-matter discussed. And what sad questions they are! Look at the Eleven in view of the topics being discussed — racism, revolution, abortion, pollution, marriage. These are momentous events, those are the questions. That is what these students are essaying to know about such issues.

Even sadder is the case of the other classrooms, where no question at all is asked while discussing capital punishment, divorce and child custody, nationalism and war, life after death, reverse discrimination (favoring a minority over the majority), public aid to religious schools, foreign aid to poor countries, socially deviant behavior (e.g., alcoholism), self-concept, graphology and horoscopes, sexual attitudes and behavior, animal intelligence, personality traits, and the rest. It is as if nothing about any of these issues were in question for the students.

Of course, like other everyday speakers, the students also use other interrogative strategies. These are not inquiries about the subject-matter but procedural, conversational, and rhetorical devices. For example:

Procedural: 'Is this going to be on the test?'
Conversational: 'What? — I didn't hear.'
Self-answered: 'One day, what did they do? — put restrictions on everybody!'
Rhetorical: 'I don't think we should help them, there's problems in our own country — why should we help another country?'

The first of these kinds is the most strategic, as students effectively use them to solve student problems — to execute routine and to bargain or negotiate over status and obligations as students. The last type is the most common, as students use them to express some feeling or to make some point. They are not questions but statements. Indeed, the common response to them is never an *answer* but 'Good point' or 'Yeah', but . . .' Altogether these other interrogative strategies accounted for six per cent of student talk. The Eleven Questions accounted for one.

It is a fact that these students had many more questions in their minds. And it is true that some of the unspoken questions will tacitly be answered by something said by somebody else as the discussion proceeds. In that same way, a question might come to our mind during a lecture, only to be answered in the next part of the lecture. But all of that is beside the point of teaching and learning in this case before us.

This is a case of spoken classroom interaction. The very proceedings are back-and-forth talk between teacher and students. That means, from the point of view of teaching and learning, that the questions are sensibly to be spoken. Otherwise it is pointless to proceed by spoken interaction — a lecture would do, or demonstration, or seatwork. The purpose for installing interaction in the first place is frustrated by the non-asking.

The interaction in this case is discussion. That means that questions rightly arise — for something is at issue — and that the questions are rightly to be shared. It is a failing, from the point of view of discussion, for a participant not to speak his mind on the issue, by withholding his questions instead of contributing them. The alibi is that some people learn just by listening and following along. That may be a good line for participating in other processes but in a discussion it defines non-participation. Not to ask is not to join in the discussion.

Further, the activity at hand is pedagogy, not some other activity. Some unspoken questions may be answered, others are not; in either case the answering is accidental. That frustrates the essence of pedagogical activity, which is to act with intention to teach and with the aim that the student learn that which is being taught. The non-asking vitiates the activity of teaching, turning it into something else.

Finally, pedagogy is planned behavior that is adjusted in the process of enacting it. For not knowing the questions in students' minds, the teacher can neither plan nor act in accordance. And in the process he cannot know whose questions are being answered and not, and which ones. He will not know the state of mind of the people whom he is teaching, and he will not know what they are learning as he is teaching them. When students do not ask questions, both teaching and learning suffer.

The whole class might just as well go to a movie. This is a place

11

where people sit silently and let one or another of the cinematic happenings accidentally strike this or that interest of this and that spectator in the audience. The case before us occurs in a classroom. The classroom process is interactive discussion. The activity is teaching and learning. On these counts it is nonsense for us to enter-tain the value of tacitly answering by accident some one or another unspoken question in the mind of this or that student, all the while not intending to do that and not knowing that it is being done.

In this case it only makes sense for students to ask their questions aloud. Nonetheless the case of the Eleven Student Questions shows them to have little actual place in classroom discourse.

Constraints of discourse

It is normal for students not to ask questions. And it is understand-able. Students have every good reason but one not to ask about things they want to know or to understand regarding the subject matter being taught to them. Most odds are against their asking. Hence when a student does ask a question it is an exceptional event, like the Eleven Student Questions.

We do well to appreciate right from the start that there are many factors, powerful ones, accounting for the singular rarity of student questions. Although these factors all operate within the classroom, not all of them originate in the classroom; nor are the more powerful ones located within the student or the teacher. There are systematic conditions, for but one example of a kind, describing such things as structures of society and schooling, socialization into institutional and situational authority roles. There are other conditions too, not springing from the classroom but impinging upon it. And there are still other conditions within school and classroom apart from factors of teacher and students. There is the curriculum itself, for example, the nature of the subject-matter and the character of materials and textbooks; and the whole complex of ways that *other* classrooms proceed with these students when they are not in our own little class time.

So we shall keep in mind for the moment that it would be a mistake for us to say, 'Well, why doesn't the *teacher* do something to change all of that?' as well as to say, 'What's the matter with these *students?*'

Among all of the factors involved we shall for the moment examine only the constraints of classroom discourse. Our effort will be to gain an appreciative understanding of how these constrain student questions, so as to start us wondering about ways to improve the remedial status of student questions in our classroom. There may not be much that we can actually do about that.

Basically, we find just what the students find — that there is little room in the discourse for students to ask questions. They understandably do not ask many questions because student questions are fairly excluded by the cycles, rules, and norms of classroom discourse.

Cycles of interaction

The way that classroom interaction normally turns leaves little room for a student to ask a question. It is understandable, then, that students who have questions in mind find it hard to fit a question into the ongoing cycle. As for the teacher, he would have to think to stop everything in order to let a student start in with a question, yet the teacher has no reason to think to stop, since no one seems to have a question. Everyone is busily engaged in the ongoing interaction.

When teacher and students are busily talking back and forth, the cycle of talk is closed to all but student *answers*. That is because the cycle typically begins with a teacher question. It then turns tightly from (a) teacher question to (b) student answer to (c) teacher evaluation of answer *plus* next question. In their one turn, students can do nothing but answer; and they have no other turn at talk.

The cycle for a *student* question turns quite differently. First of all it does not begin with a student question. Like any subordinate in other social contexts, the student must *gain permission to ask a question*. To do that the student must first of all gain the floor. Hence before the question is even asked two exchanges are required.

1. Student bid for floor
   — Teacher nomination
2. Student request to ask
   — Teacher permission

These preliminaries are not so easy to get going, especially when you're a student. For one thing, when students are bidding for the floor they are ordinarily taken to be bidding for a chance to answer the previous question. That makes for a peculiarly awkward beginning, when a student who is called upon to answer — for that is what students do — switches things around to substitute his own question at that juncture.

But although they are hard to start, the preliminaries are smoothly

13

executed. The student might wave a hand and the teacher might nod or say the student's name. Permission to ask might be sought and granted parenthetically instead of in actual words. Everyone still knows that permission is involved. For example, one of our eleven questions begins with a non-verbal bid from the student and later continues with a non-verbal accord from the teacher:

1. (Student bid)
   — Yes, Derrick.
2. Yeah, I want to ask a question.
   — (Teacher OK)
3. What country . . .?

A more polished student might say, 'Thank you. May I ask a question?' then wait for the teacher's 'Go ahead' or 'What is it?'

After a teacher question, the next move is invariably a student answer. After a student question, the next move is invariably the teacher's but no one can predict what the move will be. It can be either a reply or a non-reply to the question.

In reply, the teacher might answer the question. Other typical replies are to put a counterquestion; to redirect the question, often reformulating it into some other question; to disparage the question or questioner; to ignore it. In a non-reply, the teacher continues as before or moves ahead irrespective of the question. Hence, one of the *least* things to occur following a student question is a reply, and one of the least replies is an answer or other response in the spirit of the asking. Thus it is that asking a question may be a dispiriting move for a student.

Let us appreciate that this is normal practice, and not only in classrooms. For instance, physicians do not answer questions from patients, nor lawyers from witnesses; adults do not answer questions from children. Social superiors *ask* questions; subordinates answer them. As for the student, we may well be thinking of this single question and this single reply, but the student has had years of experience with many teachers and questions asked by self and classmates. We, the one teacher in this room at this moment, pale by comparison.

After a student answer, the next move is invariably the teacher's evaluation of the answer plus next question. After a teacher answer to a student question, the next move invariably belongs to the teacher. The teacher may at option allocate this turn to the student who asked the question; yet the student cannot use this turn to evaluate the answer, only to acknowledge it. The student can say 'oh' or 'thank you' or 'I see' and the like, but not 'yes' or 'right' or 'good' and the like. More typically the teacher retains the floor and, having answered or otherwise replied (or not) to the question, goes on to make his next move. Typically the next move is another teacher question, again beginning the tight three-step cycle:

1. Teacher question
2. Student answer
3. Teacher evaluation plus question

By entire contrast to this neat, unstoppable mechanism, the cycle for a student question turns uncertainly at every step, from parenthetical beginnings to optional endings.

1. (Student bid
   — Teacher nomination)
2. (Student request to ask
   — Teacher permission)
3. Student question
4. Teacher move
   a. Reply (optional)
   b. Non-reply
5a. Student acknowledgement (optional)
5b. Teacher move (question)

Rules of talk

Talk in classroom is governed by rules. The rules are not written but everyone knows them. Even very young pupils can tell you what they are, for the rules are quickly established at the very onset of schooling and violations are sharply pointed out. That is, everyone acts as if they know the rules. These fairly rule out student questions.

Fragile as the cycle is that involves a student question, and tentative of start, it takes remarkable tact and delicacy to find a suitable place for it to begin with. Not only does the ongoing cycle leave no room for a student question, the rules governing the discourse hardly permit it at all. Naturally, no one would dream of instituting a rule against student questions; everyone just acts as if there were a rule against them.

The general rule is 'one speaker at a time'. That means that a student may not interrupt the speaker, whether teacher or student, with a question. A superordinate rule holds that 'teacher talks at any

15

time'. That means that the teacher can interrupt the speaker, typically with a question.

Another way of putting it is that the teacher always has the floor. The next turn at talk belongs to the teacher, not to some student. That means that a student cannot take it to ask a question, for example. Indeed, the present turn at talk also belongs to the teacher, even when a student is speaking; the teacher has *allocated* the turn to the student, and can take it back at any time.

Unlike other conversations, where speakers negotiate turns and topics, in classroom discourse the turns are allocated by the one speaker, the teacher, who designates both the next speaker (whether teacher or student) and the topic. That means that a student does not, as a *rule*, just enter at some point with a question. The turns are already taken, the speaker and topic already designated; the cycle of moves already follows in step; students are already giving answers in their turn. Amidst all of this, it is a feat for a student to ask a question.

The corollaries to these rules hold that students do not have a right to speak. They must wait to be designated. When designated, they have the obligation to speak as designated, addressing the teacher and the topic specified. Generally, that means to answer the teacher's question and then stop, awaiting the evaluation of the answer plus next question.

In order for a student to ask a question, then, he must first *locate an appropriate juncture*; make a bid to talk; gain the floor; obtain permission to ask and, probably, to change the topic. That kind of move, in this kind of discourse, requires certain dynamics which is the reverse of the ongoing dynamics: not passivity, reactivity, expectancy and dependence, but student initiative, independence, energetic action, even aggression. All of that is contrary to habit. And it is against the norm.

Norms of behavior

These are even more faintly written than the rules of talk, but they are more powerfully enjoined. No norms support the student in the act of asking. Powerful norms inside the classroom and out discourage it. Although the norms are unspoken, the social reactions to the question bespeak what they are.

Even when a student has correctly followed all the rules and aptly entered the cycle of interaction, he must still, so it seems, ask just the right question in just the right way at just the right time. For example, the student must not ask a question too soon or too late.

Otherwise he will hear, ''We'll get to that later' or 'But we already had that!' The student must contrive to ask a question to which nearly everyone does *not* know the answer. Otherwise he will hear on all sides sighs and murmurs of 'What a dumb question!' and worse. One strategy is therefore to deprecate self in the asking, as if the question were not serious and probably out of place. 'I was just wondering', starts one of our Eleven, 'like — I dunno, this might be kinda dumb and stuff — but OK, like . . .'. Also the student must take care not to ask one question too many, i.e., two.

These examples are enough to indicate that, howsoever brave the venture, a student's question is widely expected to meet with negative reactions of various kinds on the part of students as well as teacher. A negative reaction may include any of the non-replies and most of the replies from the teacher, and quiet or loud disparagement from classmates — including what they will *think* of me!

It is *anti-normative* to display ignorance in school, to show perplexity, incomprehension, and need in the asking — especially when the matter is so simple and you seem to be the only one in the room who still does not understand! Further, in some classrooms, it is anti-normative to display interest in the subject-matter or the teacher. From long experience, most poignantly in the earliest years of schooling, watching what happens to self and others who ask questions, students have reasonably drawn the appropriate lesson: *'Don't ask questions'*.

The lesson is reinforced daily outside of school, save in the rarified experience of intimacy or the expensive experience of therapy. Thus powerful social forces inside and outside the classroom, involving peers as well as teacher, heart as well as mind, status as well as speech, cycles and rules and norms of discourse, dynamics of role and years of experience, marshall against the lone child before you at the moment who has a question in mind to ask. Little wonder that students go on to ask so few questions in our classroom.

Students have every good reason but one not to ask the questions that occur to them. That one reason is mastery of the world through knowledge and understanding. For the process of asking a question eventuates in learning.

THE PROCESS OF QUESTIONING

The process of questioning describes this event: 'a person asks a question.' No one knows how the process actually goes. Let us picture it to ourselves in terms broad enough to encompass most of what must be involved.

We will follow the process through four moments from start to finish. One crucial moment is when the person asks the question. Other moments come before and after the asking. The final moment follows upon the answering. That is the moment of learning.

Figure 2.1 reproduces the process, showing these moments with their events and movements in a hypothetically smooth way. As we follow along we can think of our students going through this process: 'A student asks a question.' But we do well or even better to bear ourselves uppermost in mind: 'I ask.'

Perplexity

The main event at the start is the experience of perplexity. That is the precondition of questioning and thus the prerequisite for learning. Questioning still might not follow, nor learning; without perplexity they cannot follow.

Perplexity is an organismic experience, felt in the body as well as the mind. It shows, too. We display some unease, restlessness, or discomfort when perplexed; a furrowed brow, a scratched head, a purse of the lips; we might bite fingernails and tear out hair. These and all manner of 'body language' signal above all to self that over *some* matter, pressing or fleeting, one is experiencing *a degree*, minor or great, of doubt, wonderment, ignorance, bafflement, incomprehension, uncertainty, puzzlement — perplexity. Only in that perplexed condition can a question arise.

Perplexity does not occur of itself. It is the main event of the moment but not the first. At the very start there is some percept, 'P' (Figure 2.1). We perceive something, a phenomenon or proposition P. (An account of why we perceive it in the first place, rather than overlook it as we do with thousands of others, lies outside of the depicted process of questioning.)

Next we introduce P into our scheme of things — other P's in our organized experience. When our scheme does not readily accommodate P, we have a disjunction between the new P_1 and selected previous ones, P_2. Things don't go together in the complex of propositions describing our knowledge, or things don't go smoothly in the range of phenomena describing our action. For example, we might have a goal and P_1 emerges as an obstacle; we might hold an opinion and P_1 enters to contradict. The terms encompass any kind

Figure 2.1: The process of questioning ('A student asks a question')

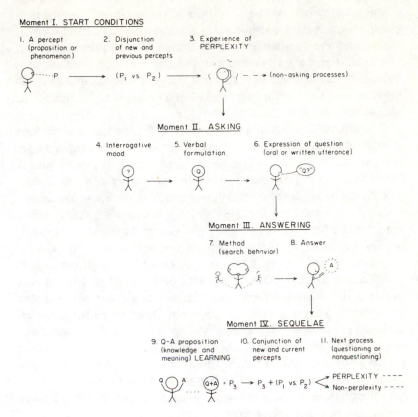

Moment I. START CONDITIONS

1. A percept (proposition or phenomenon) 2. Disjunction of new and previous percepts 3. Experience of PERPLEXITY

$(P_1 \text{ vs. } P_2)$ — — → (non-asking processes)

Moment II. ASKING

4. Interrogative mood 5. Verbal formulation 6. Expression of question (oral or written utterance)

Moment III. ANSWERING

7. Method (search behavior) 8. Answer

Moment IV. SEQUELAE

9. Q-A proposition (knowledge and meaning) LEARNING 10. Conjunction of new and current percepts 11. Next process (questioning or nonquestioning)

$(Q+A) = P_3 \longrightarrow P_3 + (P_1 \text{ vs. } P_2)$ ⟨ PERPLEXITY - - - -
Non-perplexity - - - -

of disjunction between any percepts. The disjunction describes something that we do not know or understand. The experience of perplexity ensues, whereupon a question may arise.

Asking

The main event in this moment is asking a question. But it is the least event of all to follow upon perplexity, for in the majority of cases a multitude of non-asking events will follow. Rather than go on to ask a question we may, for example, distract ourselves, dismiss or suppress the experience, settle for less, resign ourselves, give up, and so on. (An account of these other strategies lies apart from the depicted process.)

19

In the case when a question does follow, the process moves from the experience of perplexity through to the expression of a question (Figure 2.1). First, on the condition of perplexity an interrogative mood arises. Next a question emerges and assumes verbal form in mind. Then the question appears in oral or written utterance to self or others. These events do not proceed of their own, of course, but through our agency and intervention. We get ourselves into an interrogative mood and settle in it; we select a question and formulate it; we utter the question.

The last move in forming a question is the hardest, and the one least frequently taken. Fully 95 per cent of the questions that we have in mind to ask we never go on to utter. As before, we may think better of it and follow one of the numerous other paths available. These include keeping quiet and giving off that we know and understand. If we speak, our favoured strategy is to ask another question than the one we have in mind. In not asking the question in mind, we and our students have every good reason but one. For, the act of asking can be a formidable one, especially in classrooms.

When we do follow through with the process and go on to ask the question that we have formulated in our mind, our act bespeaks many things other than the question itself. These are called *presumptions of questioning*. By asking the question we hold forth our commitment to the genuineness, accuracy, or truth of these presumptions. We almost state them as we ask. And in asking a question of someone, we invite our interlocutor to join us in these presumptions — to believe them, and to believe that we believe them. The self that asks communicates as follows:

1. *Ignorance.* I am in a state of not-knowing, and I realize that I do not know.
2. *Perplexity.* I am experiencing perplexity (puzzlement, uncertainty, etc.) as a consequence of not-knowing.
3. *Need.* I feel a necessity to know.
4. *Desire.* I aspire to know.
5. *Belief.* I commit myself to the truth of the question. (I believe that its presuppositions are true, its words are as I intend them, etc.).
6. *Faith.* I am confident that the unknown is knowable.
7. *Courage.* I venture to face the unknown and its consequences both within myself and the world.
8. *Will.* I resolve to undertake to know.

These are not trifles to hold forth in a classroom (or elsewhere). Little wonder that we and our students so rarely go on to ask the question that began in our ignorance and perplexity. Yet the question promises to confer knowledge and understanding, eventuating in learning. That is just the question to ask in a schoolroom.

Answering

The next moment proceeds in complement to the asking. There are only two events — method and answer.

Method is that which the questioner does in address to the question. It is search behavior, systematic or not. The student may have recourse to self, searching his knowledge and experience to recall, to deduce or to construct an answer. He may turn to the teacher or to the other students in class, or yet to parents, friends and other likely outsiders. He may turn to the textbook, the library, a computerized information system. He may have recourse to observation and experiment, or take other action on the world.

Answer is that which is yielded by method and adduced to the question. Anything at all may have the character of answer in complement to the question — actions, things, feelings, information of all sorts — according as will resolve the asking. None of these is answer in itself. Answer is a character that accrues to them as they stand in relation to the question.

Having construed the answer, the questioner conjoins it with the question. Now he enters the moment of learning.

Learning

Learning follows in the final moment. After the answer there are three events (Figure 2.1). First and foremost there is now no longer a question that is outstanding or an answer remaining but a new production. This is the proposition that is formed of question plus answer. That is knowledge. Knowledge consists of question-answer propositions. This proposition further holds meaning and understanding. These inhere in the relation between the two complements that are made to form the proposition; they can figuratively be located in the hyphen of 'question-answer'.

This question-answer, as a proposition, represents a new 'P' in our perception. The next event introduces this new percept, P_3, into our scheme of things, a scheme that includes for some moments now our original percept P_1 and previous percepts P_2. We now have a conjunction formed of P_3 as one term, with the other term the earlier disjunction of P_1 versus P_2.

With the third and last step we may find ourselves back at the start. For the last moment fades into the first moment of some new process, whether of non-questioning or of questioning, according to the resolution of the relations obtaining between the conjoined percepts. For example, these may next serve as the presupposition to a further question.

For the moment we are left with the question-answer proposition that is our knowledge of this matter, and the question-answer relation that is our understanding of it. These as our possessions are learning. In that way the process of questioning eventuates in learning.

This process makes plain to us that the moments of questioning are apt times for teaching. Student questions make the perfect opening for teaching to enter as well as for learning to ensue.

Every time a student question arises, a child's mind opens to learning. This is the perfect opening for teaching. For one thing, the actions of child and teacher now join in pursuit of the same objective, learning. For another, the student's question serves the very purpose of teaching. It makes an opening that reveals everything necessary for pedagogical appreciation and intervention.

In asking the question the student makes a display of self. He exhibits his state of mind, his dispositions of character, and the dynamics of his relation to the world. These invite teaching. They give us to understand and appreciate this child, then to move in aptly to instruct him.

The question that is asked *exhibits the child's state of mind over the subject matter in question*. It opens to view the present and future complex of his knowledge and understanding. The presuppositions of the question show us the world as he knows it; the possible answers show us the world he is coming to know — the world he anticipates knowing and envisages as possible to know. Via the question the child is asserting the truth of some propositions and is projecting some eventual question-answer proposition. Having appreciated these, the teacher might move to correct the one and enhance the other, for example by helping the student to reformulate the question.

The act of asking *exhibits the child's dispositions of character*. These are the cognitive, affective, and behavioral propensities entailed in the presumptions of questioning — realization of ignorance, experience of perplexity, felt necessity to know, aspiration to know, commitment to the truth, confidence in the knowable, venture to face the unknown, resolve to undertake to know. Having appreciated these as they hold in the present case, the teacher can move to supplement and to sustain them, then to act upon them.

Finally, the very asking of a question *exhibits the dynamics of this child's relation to the world*. Not only does the question reveal his complex of knowledge and understanding of the subject matter; and not only does the questioning reveal his cognitive, affective, and behavioral propensities towards it. The event of asking the question makes of itself a vortex of learning dynamics — attending and thinking, readiness and motivation, participation and action. These are the very processes which educators otherwise labor to instill into the young. Here they are found in the very event of the child's asking a question. For his attention has already been engaged, his thinking already stimulated; readiness is in evidence, motivation in force; participation has been joined and action taken. Inquiry is under way and learning is sought.

It is a momentous event that faces us when a child asks a question. This is the moment of teaching. If we but step in with care, learning will follow in the next moments.

But none of this is of any use to teaching or to learning if no question is asked in the first place. And students do not ask questions in normal practice — or normally few students and few questions. Therefore the pedagogy of student questions enjoins us first to act in favor of their asking.

THE PEDAGOGY OF STUDENT QUESTIONS

The essential scheme of pedagogy is to devise action in favor of students' asking of questions in the first place. A subsequent scheme would devise suitable action to make use of the questions for further purposes of teaching and learning. Here we will design only the first and essential scheme.

In favor of student questions we as teachers can take action before, during, and after the student asks a question. First we provide for student questions. Next we welcome them when they come. Then we sustain them in the asking (Figure 2.2).

Figure 2.2: Pedagogy of student questions

```
Provide for Student Questions
   1. Make systematic room for them
   2. Invite them in
   3. Wait patiently for them
Welcome the Question
Sustain the Asking
```

Provide for student questions

To provide for student questions is to dispose the conditions under which they can arise and be expressed. Among all conditions, only certain ones are at our disposal as a teacher; and these we can dispose only to a certain point. Beyond our reach, for example, are all manner of conditions that locate within the categories of the milieu, the subject-matter, the student group, and the individual student. Surely these will not dissipate at our command — as if we could just say, 'Any questions?' and see students rise up to ask.

The one set of conditions more readily at our disposal is located within our own category, the teacher. Here we have our cognitive, affective, and behavioral dispositions affecting student questions one way or the other. If we are negatively disposed, we prevent student questions. If our disposition is positive, we cannot produce student questions but we will have provided for them as best *we* can.

We can enhance student questioning by some of the things that we think, feel, and do. The doing comes after. We might much prefer to start with some useful technique, but none exists in the absence of correct notions and good attitudes about student questions. Moreover, our little tricks are child's play in face of the mighty conditions beyond our reach.

Much depends on our *notions* about questions and their role in teaching and learning. Correct notions will not ensure that students ask questions but an uninformed view will surely see to it that they do not. Here, for example, we can study and learn about questions — what they are, how they function, and so forth. We can construct an understanding of the process of asking a question, figuring out what starts the process, how it continues, and so forth. Every point suggests techniques for practice. If we grasp the point aright, any of us can devise suitable techniques; without this grasp, any technique will be unsuitable.

Much also depends on our *attitudes* towards student questions. If we are indifferent or inimical, we will hear none. If we hold benevolent attitudes we may still hear none, for we further need to take right action. But we will have cleared away one major obstacle to student questions, while providing one good ground for them to appear. It is a matter of fact, not one of moral exertion, that we are either convinced or not of the signal value of student questions, and not of student questions in the abstract and the ideal but in the concrete and actual particulars before us. Many teachers aver the value of student questions while acting to prevent them in their classroom, wittingly or not, or doing nothing to encourage them. An easy way for us to discover our attitudes in practice is to count (*not* to estimate) the student questions asked in our classroom, and to record (not to recall) the moves that we made after the asking.

In addition to holding correct notions and good attitudes, we can take *right actions*. As before, wrong actions will prevent student questions but right actions may not produce them. At this preliminary stage, where no question has yet been asked, we can take three actions to provide for student questions.

Make room for them

Some room must be made, for normally there is no room for student questions in the ongoing discourse. Since the discourse proceeds systematically — cycles, rules, norms — systematic room must be made; and since everyone is long-conditioned to the systematic discourse, students must learn this new part of the system.

The single most effective act that we can take, and the most systematic one, is *to stop asking questions*. We make systematic room for student questions by stopping our own questioning at selected points, for selected times or activities, or by asking fewer questions overall. It is an irremovable fact of classroom life that when the teacher is asking questions the students cannot ask questions. There is a strict correlation between teacher and student questions, and it is a negative one: the more questions the teacher asks, the fewer questions the students ask. Students have no opportunity to ask and, more significantly, no dynamics that would lead them to ask.

Naturally, we would not expect our mere and sudden stoppage to release a flood of student questions. For one thing, the dynamics of passivity, dependence, and reactivity remain from years of schooling and they are being sustained daily in other classes that the students attend. For the moment all that we are doing is making some room for their questions.

25

Invite them in

The crucial act is to make room. Then we invite student questions in. They will enter hesitantly at first. Their way may be smoothed by various mechanisms and techniques that are easy to devise once we understand and appreciate student questions. (Many examples are given in the chapters on recitation and discussion.) But to invite is less a matter of technique than of our attitude. And an inviting act is more a matter of how the recipient perceives the invitation. Whatever we choose to do to invite student questions, we must first make sure that we ourselves intend to invite them and then we must make sure that the students find our act inviting.

Wait patiently for them

This act is not mysterious in attitude or ambiguous in meaning. It is literal. To wait is to produre in silence through a time; patiently is contented expectancy. We will have to wait for student questions to come, and we do well to await them patiently. They will come in time, over the course of a few months as well as within a few minutes. To help us wait on the spot, the chapter on discussion proposes the use of deliberate silence (pp. 162–167). For example, you can sing 'Baa baa, black sheep' to yourself while you wait for some venturesome soul to ask a question. Otherwise you will undoubtedly rush in with a question of your own. Not waiting patiently for student questions proves to everyone the character of your 'invitation' and the capacity of the 'room' you make for student questions in this classroom.

These are the three *generic* things to do in providing for student questions. There are hundreds of specific ways to enact them. To help us to appreciate the kinds of things involved, here are a dozen and more general ways of providing for student questions over a range of classroom activity.

1. Sometime during the *first class session* of a new course (and again later), invite the students to write down three of the questions they most assuredly have in mind about the subject matter of the course (not about the class procedure). These are the things that they are wondering about, have no idea of, always wished to know, and so forth.

Give the students time to summon and write the questions. Then take time to *hear* as many questions as will be spoken. Rather than answering any, respond to each in the spirit of the asking. For instance, repeat the question to make sure you understand it and what lies behind it; relate it to a previous question; express appreciation

26

of the question, as something worthy of wondering about; thank the student.

Collect and study the questions to get an initial sense of the students. Then make a list of the questions and distribute the list at the start of the next session, for all to see the many interesting questions in this class. Particularly for being naive questions, they are useful for teaching and learning.

Enact this procedure regularly at the start of a new unit in the course, a new topic, a new reading or story, a movie or field trip. And perhaps establish it as the regular first activity of each class session. For instance, it is useful to teaching as well as to learning to hold the question-period *before* the lecture, rather than desultorily after.

2. Base a *recitation*, or some part of it, on student questions. Have students prepare questions and then arrange for them to ask and answer in class while you listen and intervene as appropriate. (Details are in the chapter on recitation, pp. 103–110.)

3. During a *discussion*, at the specific juncture where a student has just said something, invite students to ask a question related to the previous contribution. That is to use student questions as a specific alternative to teacher questions at this juncture. (Details are in the chapter on discussion, pp. 154–158.)

4. Teach students to take a 'questioning' approach to *reading and studying*, asking questions of the subject matter and their understanding of it. Have them write their questions down on the textbook page, in a notebook or log or on a list, as part of their regular study assignment.

5. Base the *test or examination*, or some part of it, on student questions. At selected points during the unit, have each student prepare a number of written questions about the lessons and assignments to date. Duplicate their lists and arrange a group or whole-class activity to address those questions. For instance, various students can explore with a given student his particular questions that they had not thought of, do not understand, or cannot answer. You the teacher point out the questions that strike you as useful or important, and you suggest reformulations, related questions, and the like.

A selected number of student questions can then be publicly identified as the pool from which the test questions will be drawn. Half of the exam, say, might be composed of student questions; either of various students' questions, or the questions of the individual student. An individualized exam can be formed by giving back to each student his own developed and revised list of questions, which the teacher has reviewed as part of his preparing the examination. From this list, now the exam paper, the student can select a specified number of questions to answer, or he can be set to answer specified questions (e.g., circled by the teacher).

That assures both individual and group study of the subject-matter in a developing way over time; an active and comprehensive review of the material studied; and an examination fairly based on what the students have studied and actually know.

6. Ten further activities are the Practical Exercises at the end of this chapter. These are provisions made for you, as student of this subject matter, to ask questions to understand and to practise this matter — which happens also to be student questions. Hence they may be useful ways for you, as teacher, to provide for student questions.

But none of the 15 activities listed here are the things that must or should be done; they are *instances* of the kinds of thing to do — ways of providing for student questions. It is the providing which is the key, and provision is always particular to purpose in circumstances. Otherwise the thing that is done may not provide for student questions.

To provide for student questions, first make systematic room for them in the discourse, next invite them in, and then wait patiently for them. They will surely come — unless of course your notions, attitudes, and actions are to the contrary: you conceive that student questions play little role in teaching and learning; you feel that their questions aren't the right ones to ask; you don't have quite the time for them now as you cover the material; and so forth. When a student question does come the next right act is to welcome it.

Welcome the question

During the asking, the single thing we have to do is to welcome the question. This move is of surpassing importance because it teaches the students whether or not they are actually to ask questions in this class. It is a particularly crucial move when the first students begin to ask and when the student first begins to ask.

The act of welcoming is a matter of tact and delicacy, requiring considerable discipline of our pedagogical behavior. In deciding just how to embody the act of welcoming, we do well to anticipate its meaning as perceived by the *student* (and observant classmates). All we have to do is to imagine how our reactions might be perceived from their point of view, as welcoming or not.

A welcoming reaction communicates to the student: 'You are acting rightly and commendably in asking a question', and goes on to specify: '— and in asking this very question which you are now asking.' For, if we do not welcome this very question that this student is asking, we reject the student's *act* of asking. Other students will take note. They will form this rule: 'In this class you are supposed to ask questions but you are not supposed to ask your question.' As a result, students will not ask their questions.

Yet, since it is also the rule in this class to ask questions, students will learn to ask those questions which you want them to ask, whatever these are. It will take the students some time to discern, through trial and grievous error, which particular questions you find apt, timely, smart, thoughtful, surprising, stimulating. Some of the students will eventually discover the formula; these will be the good students who ask good questions. Those questions will not be the students' questions, and no other students will even dream of asking their own inept, untimely, dumb, thoughtless, dull, and tiresome questions. But students are accustomed to having to do odd things in the course of schooling. In the normal case they learn not to ask questions. In this case the odd thing to do is to ask someone else's questions and not your own.

Not to welcome the very question that is being asked is contrary pedagogy. It frustrates learning and the very purpose of this teaching.

One good way to welcome student questions is *to listen and to attend* to them as they are being asked. That gives off the rightful impression that student questions are important events in this classroom. It is as if the act of asking were worthy of note and the question deserving of respect. It matters not a whit what the question is. It is not a matter of how the question strikes us personally or even professionally as a specialist in this subject matter. ('At last an interesting question!'). It is a matter of pedagogy.

We *as teachers* accord importance to these events, and not because of their content but for their portent. Here is a child whom we are to teach, and this child is asking a question. This is the moment we have been waiting for, the perfect opening for teaching. The child is exhibiting to us the complex of his knowledge and understanding of the subject matter in question, together with his cognitive, affective, and behavioral propensities towards it. He is dynamically aroused and active as a learner — in his attention and

29

thinking, readiness and motivation, participation and energetic action. Inquiry is under way, and learning is being sought. Whatever the question that is being asked at the moment, attentive listening is the pedagogical behavior that is called for, for we as teachers are genuinely impressed with the important act that is going on before us in this moment.

The opposite impression is easily given. Although they may not be talking, many teachers are seen not to listen or to attend to student questions while they are being asked. Instead, they are observed to consult their notes, to glance at the clock, to pace about, to collect papers, to store paraphernalia. We might choose to discipline ourselves to look intently at the person who is asking and in silent appreciation to open our senses to his meaning, as if someone and something significant were at issue here, and as if the issues were at the very heart of teaching and learning. That is to welcome a student question. Of course, if you think it's a silly question you'll do something else about it. And that will be the end of that, and the other questions too.

Sustain the asking

After the question has been asked, the one thing to do is to sustain the asking. The last thing is to answer it.

To sustain means to nurture the act of asking and to keep the question and the questioner alive. Inquiry is the event of the moment, and it is a rare and fragile occurrence. Whatever we do should be directed to sustaining inquiry now that it has emerged, and to sustaining the student in his venture to inquire. These are the events of significance, even if the question concerns 1066 and all that.

Yet it seems only polite and furthermore educationally sound for us to answer the question. But it is a pedagogical blunder.

To answer the question is to blunder on various grounds. First it fails to sustain the crucial events of the moment — the asking, the asker, and the asked. The effect is to make of these nothing more important than a moment's passing, something to pass over in the rush to the more important matters — answers, certainty, determinacy, assertions, solutions, quiescence. That may come later. At the moment what is of importance is the experience of ignorance and perplexity, the desire to know, the courage to ask, the venture to inquire. These are the things deserving of sustenance. The teacher's answer only cuts them short.

30

Second, that student or some other may well arrive at the answer. That is to follow through with the process of questioning — pursuing a method, deriving an answer, forming a question-answer proposition. That is learning how to learn. Better to help the students through the process than to foreshorten it for them.

Third, the spoken question is rarely the question in mind; we would be answering the wrong question! That is the case with most other people, not only with students. With students it is even more the case because almost by definition they have less facility in expressing their mind, especially their confusion and perplexity, still less in the bursts of speech allotted to them in normal classroom discourse, and all the less during discussions of issues unfamiliar and complex to their mind. Better to find out what question is being asked in the first place.

Fourth, the question in the student's mind, spoken or not, is often a mistaken one. The student may be confused not in the first place about the question but about some prior point that he misheard, misunderstood, misinferred, on the basis of which he asks the question. But he does not know that he is confounded about the prior point; he is clear about that but confused about the question. We would then be giving a correct and direct but misleading and meaningless answer to a question that is mistaken to begin with. And we would *not know* that we have left the student even more confounded, nor would he himself suspect that from our ready, authoritative answer. Better to explore the grounds of the question.

Finally, to answer is to blunder on the grounds of not pausing to appreciate what the question reveals about this student's state of mind — his knowledge and understanding of the subject matter past and future. We would answer without insight into this student whom we are to teach. Better to take this moment to appreciate the person who asks.

Let us turn these grounds around and restate some positive actions to take in the moment after the student has asked a question. It is only a matter of a few seconds or so, an exchange or two. But time is not of the essence at this moment. Sustaining the asking is.

1. *Reinforce and reward the experience of perplexity and the expression of inquiry*. Support it as normative in this classroom, laud it as the precondition to learning. In most classrooms the norm is placid, unruffled procession through the subject matter. Perplexity is deliberately skirted as an undue disturbance to the students' rightful state of mind. It only upsets and confuses them, after all.

2. *Help the student and classmates to devise a method in address*

to the question. Teach them that they can empower themselves to know. Discipline yourself against the appeal to your authority and help them to grow up.

3. *Find out the question that the student has in mind to ask*, helping him to formulate and express it aright.

4. *Examine together the grounds of the question*. Discover its presuppositions and how the student understands them. Explore the presumptions of asking and how you and the student mutually believe them to hold in this case.

5. *Appreciate the student's state of knowledge revealed by the question*. Look back to the knowledge that lies behind the question and look forward to the kind of knowledge that it promises in answer, seeing the world as the student knows it and envisages it to be knowable. Correct the one and widen the other by helping him to reformulate the question.

These are five general ways of sustaining the asking. At a later moment you might answer the question if appropriate.

One specific way to start sustaining a student question is to *restate it* with praise or interest. (For goodness' sake, don't put a counter-question or throw the question back to the student!) For example, 'You're wondering if Q. Good question.' Or, 'Oh, what you want to know is Q. Yeah, that's interesting.' More often than not, the student will go on to

— *reformulate the question*: 'Well, what I meant was Q2.'
— *elaborate its grounds*: 'Yeah, because . . .'
— *devise an answer*: 'I dunno, I guess A.'

The restatement also makes of this individual's question a public contribution to other students who might join in the inquiry or at very least notice the question. (Like teachers, students do not listen when students speak.) For example, here is the exchange that followed one of our Eleven Student Questions, during a heated discussion of students' smoking privileges just revoked by the school.

S1: . . . So, does that mean if you smoke, you're not a good Christian?

T: Well, I — that's a good question.

S2: There's no sin against smoking.

T: Does that mean if you don't smoke, you're a better Christian, then?

S3: It doesn't mean you're a worse one.

S1: And just like . . . I dunno if that's Christian or not, that's what I'm saying.

S4: I remember something you said [teacher], when you were explaining Christian relationships . . . And you brought out a cigarette, . . . Same thing!

T: That's true. With that in mind . . .

In this case, sustaining the question enriched the discussion and led to further inquiry by both the questioner and classmates as well as the teacher.

These are merely examples, instances of ways to sustain the asking. The question can be a matter of fact or opinion; the teacher can restate and praise the question or take other action to sustain it. The details are not of the essence. The critical pedagogical behavior is to sustain the student and the question in the asking.

When and if informed by correct and good attitudes towards student questions, our practice then moves us to take action before, during, and after a student asks a question — to provide for student questions, to welcome the question when it comes, and to sustain the asking. There are manifold ways to enact these moves; and many clever techniques do not enact them. In general, a well-informed and positively disposed teacher like yourself can devise techniques suitable to purpose in circumstance. Broadly suitable ways to provide, welcome, and sustain student questions during recitation and discussions are illustrated in Chapters 4 and 5. Other ways are found in the Correlated Readings at the end of this chapter, and in the Practical Exercises that follow. The exercises are designed to help you as a student to use questions; they may be useful as well to help your students.

All of that is to discipline our pedagogical behavior in service of educative purpose in our classroom circumstance. We will do none of it if we think that the questions our students ask serve to little purpose. In that case, nothing at all that we do will encourage them to ask questions. Our practice will be the normal one, with the usual results in learning.

'Well, then,' proposed Socrates, 'if you should ever be charged in actual fact with the upbringing and education of these imaginary children of yours, . . . so you will make a law that they must devote themselves especially to the technique of asking and answering questions.'

— 'Yes, I will, with your collaboration.' (*Republic* VII. 534)

With no help from Socrates, children everywhere are schooled to become masters at answering questions and to remain novices at asking them. The normal practice is to induce in the young answers given by others to questions put by others. A complementary practice would induce student questions, forming their answers in the public light of joint inquiry.

Those of us who would educate the Socrates within the children before us can make of our classroom a place where they ask as well as answer questions. All we have to do is to open the grounds for student questions to arise and for learning to follow in answer.

CORRELATED READINGS

A Education

Dillon, J.T. (1981) 'A norm against student questions', *Clearing House*, *55*, 136–139 — an easy questionnaire study and discussion of why students don't ask questions, from their point of view.

Dillon, J.T. (1986) 'Student questions and individual learning', *Educational Theory*, *36*, 333–341 — a conceptual analysis of student questions (their presuppositions and presumptions), with designs for pedagogy in classrooms, reading processes, and computerized instruction.

Dillon, J.T. (In press) 'The remedial status of student questioning', *Journal of Curriculum Studies* — a review and discussion of studies, ideas, and practices that might enhance questioning by students.

Fahey, G.L. (1942) 'The questioning activity of children', *Journal of Genetic Psychology*, *60*, 337–357 — a review of the early literature on the questions of children, especially in classrooms.

Helseth, I.O. (1926) 'Children's thinking: A study of the thinking done by a group of grade children when encouraged to ask questions about United States History', *Teachers College Contributions to Education*, No. 209 — one of the oldest and best studies, recounting a teacher's year-long effort to encourage her pupils to ask questions.

Hunkins, F.P. (1976) *Involving students in questioning*, Boston: Allyn & Bacon — the only one of its kind, a manual of tips and techniques for teachers to encourage student questions.

Susskind, E. (1969) 'The role of question-asking in the elementary school classroom', in F. Kaplan and S. Sarason (eds.), *The psycho-educational clinic*, New Haven, CT: Yale; Susskind, E. (1979) 'Encouraging teachers to encourage children's curiosity', *Journal of Clinical Child Psychology*, *8*, 101–106 — a correlational study, one of the best available, plus a training study, on the questions of elementary school pupils compared to their teachers' questions.

Tamminen, K. (1977) 'What questions of life do Finnish school children reflect on?', *Learning for Living*, *16*, 148–155; Tamminen, K. (1979) 'Pupils' questions and interests: Material for problem-centered

education?', *Character Potential*, *9* (1), 5–21 — rich descriptive study
of 10,000 life questions faced by children at all levels of schooling
(elicited by projective techniques) with a proposal for basing part of the
curriculum on these questions.

van der Meij, H. (1986) *Questioning*, The Hague: SVO — the most
comprehensive source to date, with conceptions, interviews and
experiments about the questioning behavior of elementary school
children.

Wong, B.Y.L. (1985) 'Self-questioning instructional research', *Review of
Educational Research*, *55*, 227–268 — a review and discussion of
experimental studies on the effects of student questions while reading
and studying.

B Other fields

Belnap, N. and Steel, T. (1976) *The logic of questions and answers*, New
Haven, CT: Yale — a standard theory from logic, clear and simple but
formal and hard-looking, on what questions are, how they arise and
relate to answers.

Clark, M. (1972) *Perplexity and knowledge: An inquiry into the structures
of questioning*, The Hague: Nijhoff — a dense analysis, from existential
or transcendental philosophy, of what it is to be a knower and questioner,
from self's viewpoint.

Dillon, J.T. (1982) 'Problem finding and solving', *Journal of Creative
Behavior*, *16*, 97–111 — a conception of how people discover,
formulate, or create problems by contrast to solving problems (cf. asking
questions and answering questions).

Dillon, J.T. (1984) 'The classification of research questions', *Review of
Educational Research*, *54*, 327–361; Dillon, J.T. (1987) 'Questioning in
science', in M. Meyer (ed.), *Questions and Questioning*, Berlin: De
Gruyter — reviews of conceptions, studies, and practices of scientific
research as a process of questioning (cf. the questions of scientists and
scholars, the questions of children and students).

Dillon, J.T. (1983) 'The use of questions in educational research', *Educational Researcher*, *12* (9), 19–24; Dillon, J.T. (1985) 'Categories of
inquiry in Curriculum Perspectives and other journals', *Curriculum
Perspectives*, *5*, 1–5; Dillon, J.T. (1985) 'The problems/methods/
solutions of curriculum inquiry', *Journal of Curriculum and Super-
vision*, *1*, 19–26; Dillon, J.T. (1987) 'Finding the question for evaluation research', *Studies in Educational Evaluation* (in press at time of
writing) — descriptive studies, discussion, and advice on asking questions as a researcher; relations among question-method-answer.

Flammer, A. (1981) 'Towards a theory of question asking'; Flammer, A.
et al. (1981) 'Predicting what questions people ask', *Psychological
Research*, *43*, 407–420 and 421–429 — a rare theory from cognitive
psychology, with an experiment published alongside, on how people ask
questions of information.

Meyer, M. (1983) *Meaning and reading*, Amsterdam: Benjamins — an original theory of hermeneutics and literary criticism, showing how a reader understands a text by formulating the question to which it is an answer, then questioning the answer.

Olinick, S. (1954) 'Questioning and pain, truth and negation', *Journal of the American Psychoanalytic Association*, 5, 302–324 — a psychoanalysis, deep and fascinating, of the person or ego while in the act of raising a question; e.g. the questions of a patient in a psychoanalytic therapy session.

PRACTICAL EXERCISES

1. Try asking

During the next class session of some course that you are attending as a student (not this course), ask one question that perplexes you about the subject-matter being taught and studied — something that you genuinely do not understand and personally want to know. Then reflect on any aspect of interest to you about the asking — e.g. what it took for you to ask such a question; how you managed to introduce it aloud into the ongoing class; what reactions you met with or sensed from classmates and teacher.

Do it again in a subsequent class session, but push further. After the one question, try to ask a second and a third question. See if you are permitted to ask three questions in a row, or three questions over the class hour. Note the changing conditions as you ask more questions. Then formulate your sense of the norms for student questions in this classroom — who can ask, when, in which manner, how often, about what — and check your formulation with classmates.

Perhaps you and another student in this present course could do this exercise, each in a different course. Then in this class you might report and discuss your exercises, in light of this chapter.

2. Be presumptuous

Recall any two or three questions that you asked yesterday or recently in the normal course of life (outside of school). Systematically examine each question against the eight 'presumptions of questioning' in this chapter (p. 20). Describe the effect of violating the various presumptions. Estimate how many questions in everyday discourse satisfy the presumptions. Then wonder about these presumptions for student questions and educative purposes in classroom discourse.

3. Appreciate your non-asking

List out all the good reasons you as a student have for not asking questions. Be specific to you yourself, identifying your actual reasons rather than imagining the reasons for 'students' in general. Include the story of one colorful or poignant experience from previous schooling, when you asked a question or watched a classmate ask.

If some fellow students in this course also do this exercise, you can gather as a group to discuss your reasons and to enhance your appreciative understanding of why students don't ask questions.

As a useful variant of this exercise, report the confirming experiences and other sound reasons that you actually possess (vs. claim in theory) for your actual asking of questions in class.

4. Experience your perplexity

Quietly summon to yourself the question that recurrently bothers you or most concerns you about your life or the world around you. Formulate and feel the question anew.

That's all. If you like, go on to do one or another of these exercises on this perplexing question.

5. Identify your questions

Write out the various questions left in your mind after reading this chapter. For a fact you have at least three. Choose any three and rewrite them until they express just the question that is in your mind.

If your instructor and fellow students will join you, this exercise becomes more fruitful. Someone might offer to collocate the questions and circulate the list. Then the class could (a) discuss the *questions* themselves as questions; (b) answer them as a group; (c) use them to guide study and understanding of this chapter. These questions might further serve as the 'pool' of items for the course examination or test.

Plan to do this exercise after each chapter. Then the subsequent chapters will be better read, and the reading will yield better comprehension of this subject-matter.

6. Anticipate the questions

Identify the questions that this chapter did not address but should have, in your view. These are questions that you would expect or want to be answered by such a chapter, yet you find them not even treated. Now go on to anticipate the questions to be addressed in the next chapter. Write them out and keep them in mind while reading. Use them to pursue this subject matter through the class activities, further readings, and exercises.

7. Form your question-answer proposition

Formulate the single question that this chapter answers as a whole. Regard the entire chapter as an answer, and construe the question to which it stands in relation of answer. Next, formulate the chapter's answer to that question.

Then state that question-answer proposition. That gives your knowledge and understanding of this chapter. You can now state in a single sentence what this chapter says and means, to your sense.

Last, gather with fellow students (or with a congenial colleague, if you are not in a course) to hear each person's statement (viz., question-answer proposition) of what the chapter says. Discuss the different understandings that each is proposing.

The device to guide discussion is the question that is formulated by each student and by the instructor. Bear on the questions; see how they might be reformulated; see if they can be combined into a single question (then a single answer) formed and constructed by the group. The resulting question-answer proposition holds the class' knowledge and understanding, now a public possession.

As a variant of this exercise, or yet to pursue it, do it again by yourself but now on the three major sections of the chapter, one by one; on some one subheading of a major section; and on any single paragraph and sentence within. That will give you a systematically interrelated understanding of the chapter as a whole, its parts and details. You can proceed by questioning the answer in each case.

Plan to do this exercise with the next chapter but *while reading* it. Your study will be more powerful and concentrated, your learning richer and more confident. Imagine reading a whole text — a book, a story, an article — and then being able, as you will be able, to stand up and to say, at least to yourself, *what the book says*; and to say it all *in a single statement*. You might well be mistaken. But that is always the case with any reader and text. Now you have a way to know for sure what you do know; and a specific device for joining with others to share and to enhance your understanding — not to mention forming together an understanding in common.

8. Compose your view of questions

This one may be the hardest but eventually most fruitful exercise. The next chapter is on teacher questions. You may have misread part of this present chapter, for thinking of teacher questions or for substituting educational commonplaces for the views being presented. In any case, it is your view that is now at issue.

Go back to the first two paragraphs of the chapter (p. 7). Actively substitute 'teacher' for student and see what sense the paragraphs make to you. You may think that *teacher* questions stimulate thought, or lead to learning. Write your own paragraph, composing an argument or theory to express and to sustain your view of teacher questions — just as you now conceive it to be, without further study and ado. Then write a second paragraph or composition on your view of student questions. Lastly, change Figure 2.1 around or draw another, to suit your view of the questioning process.

These compositions will be the heart of your practice of questioning. As such, they are far more crucial and valuable than the composition of this chapter. Keep your compositions physically and mentally with you as you proceed to read and to study this book and to discuss it in class. Courageously revise them as your understanding changes and/or becomes clearer to you, in just the way that you freely take or leave or annotate the views in this book.

Revise and reconstruct your views several times over until in the end you are satisfied, for the moment, that these are indeed what you think and feel, know and understand about questioning and teaching.

That is what you will enact in your classroom. Then, reflecting on your practice you will continue to revise both your understanding and your practice. Doing that goes some way towards being a good questioner, a good student, and a good teacher.

9. Sustain someone's question

The next time that you are asked a question by someone undaunting, act to sustain it rather than to answer it right away. After the person asks, restate the question with interest. For example, 'You're wondering if Q. Interesting.' 'Oh, what you want to know is Q. Yeah, that's interesting.' Make sure that you *restate* the question, not change it; and in a *declarative* phrase, not a questioning tone. Note what the questioner says in reply.

10. Observe student questions

See for yourself how students ask questions in normal practice. Walk into a few classrooms where teacher and students are talking back and forth, and record the questions that students ask. Work out the frequencies and types of questions.

If you are a student now, do this exercise unobtrusively in the next few class sessions of the various courses you are taking (but not this course).

If you are presently a teacher, observe the questions asked by students in your own class. Pick your best and brightest class, if you like, on any good day. First write down your estimate of the number of questions that students usually ask during a normal class hour, together with the number of students who usually ask questions; add an estimate of the number of questions that you usually ask during an hour.

Then record the questions actually asked. Tape-record the class hour, or engage a student or two to tally and write down the questions as they are spoken by you and by students. Set up the system so as not unduly to influence your behavior. For example, tape-record a week of classes and then toss a coin to determine which tape, apart from the first and last, you will examine. Or tell the students to choose any day they like for their tally work, say between next week and the following.

Last compare the evidence and your estimates. Wonder what you can do about student questions in your classroom. This wonderment is a good question. Its answer will be found in your subsequent practice.

3

Teacher Questions

OVERVIEW

USES OF TEACHER QUESTIONS
Classroom processes
Planning processes
   Design of lesson
   Study of the subject-matter
   Preparation of activity
Evaluation processes

QUESTIONING TO PURPOSE
Pedagogical purposes
Classroom circumstances
   Learner
   Subject-matter
   Activity
   Milieu
   Result
Questioning behaviors
   Usage
   Quantity
   Kind
   Topic
   Form
   Addressee
   Timing
   Manner
   Presumptions
   Purpose

PEDAGOGY OF TEACHER QUESTIONS
Prepare the questions
    Purposes
    Preparation
Pose the questions
    Question
    Answer
    Reaction
Reflect on questions
    Assessment
    Redesign

CORRELATED READINGS

PRACTICAL EXERCISES

Figure 3.1: Questioning to purpose
Figure 3.2: Pedagogy of teacher questions

Teacher Questions

Teacher and students join in the pursuit of learning through questioning. Teacher and student questions complement one another in service of educative purposes in classroom circumstances.

The teacher's questions are pedagogical devices. Whether he is perplexed or not by the matter in question, the teacher asks with pointed interest in the answers. For the very pursuit of teaching, the teacher needs to know the student's answer and thus the student's knowledge of that which is being taught. To this end the teacher can use questions through a range of classroom processes, including lecture as well as classroom interaction. In addition, the teacher can use questions as devices for planning and for evaluating the classroom process. All of these are uses for teaching, an activity that begins and ends outside of the classroom.

The mere fact that questions can be so used signifies nothing of their good use. Any teacher can put questions to good use or ill in any activity at any moment of teaching. The use of questions can be skilful or blundering, serving to no good purpose or to contrary purpose. That which characterises good use is service to purpose in circumstance. Yet, like anyone else, teachers can with ease use questions to serve purposes other than educative ones, and effortlessly use questions contrary to circumstance even as they strive to achieve educative purposes. The principle is *to discipline pedagogical behavior in service of educative purposes in classroom circumstances*. Of itself that says little about actual practice. The practice specifies particulars of questioning behavior for particulars of purpose in circumstance.

The scheme of disciplined action for teacher questions begins and ends in acts of thought where purposes and circumstances are specified to self, so as to make apt choice among questioning behaviors. The teacher first prepares the questions, next poses them, then reflects on them. Reflection yields the understanding needed to inform further practice.

To inform our practice of teacher questions, we will first review the many *uses of questions* for the teacher while in and out of the classroom. Next we describe *questioning to purpose*, displaying the choice of questioning behaviors to suit purposes in circumstances. Then we outline the *pedagogy of teacher questions* in a generic scheme of action from which specifics of practice can be derived as suitable to purpose in circumstance. In all of these respects, an understanding of *answers* turns out to be the best practical guide to using questions.

USES OF TEACHER QUESTIONS

Questions can be put to surprising uses for teaching and learning, and not only in the classroom. To illustrate, please picture yourself while teaching in a classroom. With that picture in mind, let us see how questions are being used for almost anything that you may be doing. Then we will reveal how questions are also used while doing things that are not seen in the classroom.

Classroom processes

As you imagine yourself teaching in a classroom, you must be picturing some kind of activity or process going on. You and the students may be engaged in classroom interaction, such as recitation or discussion; in a lecture, demonstration, or other presentation; in quiet seatwork or examination. In these and still other processes you can see that questions are being used.

When you and the students are talking back and forth over the subject-matter, questions are being asked and answered. In a *discussion* of the matter, you pose the question that is at issue, to which the whole discussion represents an attempt to answer. While addressing this issue, students raise questions about aspects they do not understand, in hopes that the discussion will contribute to their forming an answer. In a *recitation* over the subject-matter, you put questions about things that you and they are presumed to know, in answer to which you discover the students' state of knowledge. Students ask further questions about things they do not know or understand well.

When students are silent and you continue to talk to the class you can deliver your *lecture* or other presentation as an answer to a question that you have devised or that they have asked.

When everyone is silent and students are doing *seatwork*, they answer questions that you have devised as suitable exercises, practice, and so forth. You can pose these orally or write them on the board or on worksheets, or you can select them from the text or workbook materials. As you walk about the room, you and individual students ask questions about the work.

Similarly, the students fall silently at work while answering questions that you have set for *examination*, on a test or quiz for the day or month.

Towards the end of the class hour you set further questions for students to answer as a *homework assignment*. You pose questions orally for them to think about, or you distribute written questions as guides for further study of today's lesson, of tomorrow's reading, or for a later examination.

As the bell rings and students file out of the room, some students approach you for *tutoring* or individual help. They and you ask and answer over the subject-matter. One student lingers a while after class, or another arrives early for the next class, for *counseling* or *guidance* over some private non-academic or scholastic matter. Again you and they ask and answer, rather briefly.

You arrange for the student to obtain more extensive guidance and counseling from others in the school, or for *individualized instruction* from programmed materials and computerized systems, where student and educative agent will exchange further questions and answers.

Just as the student departs another arrives with a package from the school office, containing multiple forms of the *standardized tests* or *questionnaires* which you are to administer on the morrow, nothing but questions for students to answer as part of assessing their academic aptitudes and achievement, vocational interests, personal attitudes, social habits, backgrounds, and anything else.

These are the uses of questions in classroom processes. But by no means does that signify good or effective use. Of itself, the use of questions serves no educational purpose. It may well be an everyday use of questions, despite being used by a teacher in a classroom. It may be an unskilled use of questions. Everything educational depends upon the good use of questions to serve purposes in circumstances. That in turn depends upon preparing the question for good use.

Hence the first use of teacher questions is not, surprisingly enough, in classroom processes. It is in the process of planning for classroom activity. Questions are useful devices for planning teaching as well as useful devices for teaching.

Planning processes

Before entering the classroom, we plan the teaching-learning activity to be enacted therein. That includes preparing the questions to be posed. Planning also involves a different, prior use of questions as devices for our planning. Hence we first use questions as devices for planning our teaching, then as devices for teaching.

We began by picturing ourselves in the midst of the classroom process. Let us now imagine ourselves engaged in the planning process, say alone at night in our home. We will need an illustration that all of us can follow, so let us imagine ourselves preparing to teach a lesson on the subject-matter of this very chapter, viz., teacher questions. We will follow ourselves through three aspects of planning — design of the lesson, study of the subject-matter, and preparation of the classroom activity.

Design of lesson

Tomorrow we will be teaching a lesson over this subject-matter; tonight we design the lesson to teach. First we ask ourselves those questions to which each part of the design will represent an answer. Then we work out the suitable answer.

For example, here is a generic design. It leads us to work out what we want our students to learn, how they are going to go about learning that, and how we are going to find out what they learn.

1. *Purpose.* What is it, exactly, that I want my students to learn tomorrow? In terms of the illustration: What do I want them to learn about teacher questions?

2. *Instruction.* (a) *student activity*: What is it that my students must do, be, have, in order to learn that which I propose they learn? (b) *teacher activity*: As a consequence of (a), what must I do in order that my students can do that which they must do in order to learn? (See answer to Q2a.)

3. *Evaluation.* How, exactly, will I know that the students have learned that which is proposed to be learned? (See answer to Q1.) How, exactly, will I discover *what else* the students have learned as a result of the activity? (See Q2ab.)

Various other schemes can be used to design a lesson. The example illustrates the use of questions in designing a lesson, whatever the scheme of the design. Suppose you are given a detailed ten-point scheme for a lesson plan; and suppose that none of the three points in this example so much as appear on the form. No matter. Formulate the question that is at issue for each of the ten points. Then fill in the answers. Otherwise you will just be filling in blanks.

Study of the subject-matter

As part of preparing for class, we study the subject-matter that is set for teaching and learning on the morrow. Here we use questions as simple and intellectually powerful devices for study.

First we take a 'questioning' approach to the study. With questions in our mind we read the textbook or materials, or we examine the other forms of the subject-matter (e.g., a movie). Second, we outline the material, identifying and arranging the questions that it answers. The result is a surer grasp of the subject plus a useful outline for our teaching of it and for the students' learning of it.

Let us take this very chapter as the subject-matter set for teaching and learning. Whether for student or for teacher, questions are useful devices for studying this subject-matter. To illustrate:

• call to mind the questions that you have about this subject-matter, to wit, teacher questions;

• feel and formulate the questions that arise to your mind about this chapter, to wit, this form of the subject-matter;

• make a question-outline of this chapter, identifying and arranging the questions that each of its parts sets out to answer. You are now reading the answers; figure out the questions. Which questions does this first part ('Uses of Teacher Questions') answer as a whole? Which questions do these subsections answer? ('Classroom Processes' and 'Planning Processes'.)

As a result, you will know this chapter and how to teach it. For instance, you will know the points that need to be corrected or supplemented in class; and you will have a list of questions to ask as a review or test over the reading.

Preparation of activity

This aspect of planning leads us to specify the classroom activity for the morrow — lecture, recitation, discussion, and so forth. Now we have to prepare the questions that are suitable to the process we plan to engage in. Let us continue to take this chapter as the subject-matter we will teach.

For a recitation, we prepare an ordered list of questions to put during a review of the subject-matter, in view of finding out what the students know of it. We order the list according to the anticipated answers and their interrelations. These we know from our study of the chapter; for example, our question-outline of it.

To illustrate: *Which ten questions do you propose to set for a recitation over this chapter?* Write down the main and subsidiary questions, then sketch out the alternative answers — the correct answer, the various incorrect ones likely, and the various acceptable answers. For Q1, we have A1, A2, A3; for Q2, A1, A2, A3. By tracing the relations among the answers we dispose the order of questions to ask. Of course, we do not know the order in which we will actually go on to ask them; our preparation disposes the questions to be asked in a suitable order. In class we may wind up asking Q5 in second place because A2 instead of A1 was given to the first question that we asked. But we are prepared to do so.

For a discussion, we prepare the question that will be at issue during the discussion. The preparation of this one question will likely take as long as preparing the ten questions for recitation. We spend time conceiving of the suitable question, formulating it aright, and writing it out several times until satisfied with its expression. The variations suggest to us the questions that are subsidiary to it, related, componential, embedded in the main question; and thus those specific questions that are likely to arise during the course of discussion.

To illustrate: *Which question do you propose for an hour's discussion over this chapter?* State only a single interrogative sentence (ending with a question mark). Please do not go on and on telling us what the question is while you figure out just what is in question, all the while changing it as you speak.

For a lecture or other presentation, we prepare the questions that our lecture will answer. That is altogether distinct from preparing what we are going to say. For first we identify the questions, then we work out what we are going to say in answer. The way to do that is to make a question-outline. As a result, the lecture proves to be a complete and coherent presentation, consisting of an ordered set of systematically interrelated question-answer propositions. That is what its character will be and how it will be received, regardless of our choice to ask the questions or not while delivering the lecture.

To illustrate: *What set of questions do you propose to answer in a lecture on this chapter?* The ordered set looks just like any outline, save that its points are questions:

    I. QUESTION
        A. Question
           1. question
           2. question
   II. QUESTION
        etc.

Preparing this outline is not the same task as making a question-outline of the chapter. In that case we know the answers and work out the questions; here we create the questions and work out the answers. But of course we may also choose to lecture directly from various texts that we have consulted in preparation, relying on the question-outline that we have made of the material while studying. By contrast, it seems odd to deliver a lecture following the outline of a chapter that both you and the students have read and outlined in preparation for the lecture. Nonetheless such oddities are normal at least at the advanced levels of schooling.

Having used questions to conceive and outline our lecture, we complete our preparation by filling in the answers. They may require further study and thought on our part, or simple recall and specification of matters we already know well. Hence the further use of questions is to discipline the character and form of what we shall actually say. We compose the suitable answer to the questions specified in our outline, then write them down:

I.   QUESTION — ANSWER
    A. Question — Answer
       1. question — answer
    etc.

This simple two-step task requires uncommon discipline. Disciplined thought and labor are involved in conceiving, formulating, and ordering the questions to be addressed, and then finding, formulating, and fitting their answers.

The great effort is to pin self down to the question, actually writing the question out and then the answer. It is much easier to imagine the question and to form an idea of the answer. Far easier still to compose a few remarks on the way to the classroom. Experienced lecturers have been observed to write the lecture out word for word. That is admirable, providing they know the question they are answering. It is enough to write the lecture out question by question.

The question-outline approach and the other question-approaches are also useful to preparing other class processes and activities — other presentations and demonstrations, movies, field-trips, and the like. In addition, they are useful for planning student assignments and practice activities — seatwork, homework, study guides, worksheets, and the like.

To illustrate: *Which three questions do you propose for a study or practice activity to follow upon the lecture/recitation/discussion that you have prepared for this chapter?* To devise these questions you will have to plan ahead and anticipate the likely state of your students after the lecture or discussion, etc. Here again questions prove useful devices for planning, and also for preparing the very questions to follow. For example, the questions which you have prepared for the lecture/recitation/discussion, together with the organization that you have given to them, point to the next sensible question for students to deal with whether they achieve all or part of the activity.

Evaluation processes

Pursuing the same line as developed thus far, we can easily see how questions are useful devices for evaluation of student learning. We can use them as a device to plan an evaluation and we can use them as the evaluation device.

For example, we can plan evaluation as an answer to the generic question: who learned what from the teaching? The design illustrated earlier specifies: How will I know that the students have learned what was proposed for learning? What else did the students learn as a result of this teaching-learning activity?

As a way of answering these questions we can formulate specific questions about the subject-matter and set these for examination, for a written or oral quiz or test, or for some other activity, project, or production of the student from which we can infer learning. The specific questions to set follow as a matter of course from the organized set of question-answers that we have laboriously prepared for the lesson; and from that part of the set which we observed to be addressed or not, and to be handled with a given degree of facility and sufficiency by various students and by the class as a whole, during the classroom process.

We can also use questions as devices to evaluate our very use of questions during these classroom processes. Here we reflect on our practice of questioning, observing and analyzing our use of questions much as a researcher might who studies our classroom. Of our questions we ask, for example: How do they work? To what extent did they serve to purpose? Which questions did we actually ask, in which manner, and to whom? We might tape-record our lesson and compare the oral questions to our written ones on the prepared list, reflecting on the choices that we made in the circumstances, and estimating the consequences. Then we can make a new design, again preparing questions for the morrow's lessons.

That is to return to the planning process, where questions are first put to good use in service of teaching and learning.

QUESTIONING TO PURPOSE

The general scheme of using questions parallels the scheme of teaching. They are schemes of action. The action begins in planning and ends in reflection.

We have just seen something of the practice of teaching. Teaching comprehends more than classroom action; it involves forethought and afterthought as well. The activity that constitutes teaching begins in an act of planning and design, continues in classroom action, and ends in a reflective act of evaluation and redesign.

The teacher's use of questioning follows a similar course. The practice involves more than the act of putting a question to a student in the classroom. It entails acting before, during, and after.

1. Planning. Our first act is to choose the question for the asking. The choice is made in favor of our purpose in our classroom circumstances.

2. Enactment. Next we put the questions in classroom action. Action is enacted choice.

3. Reflection. Then we reflect on the consequences of enacted choice.

This is the generic scheme, lacking all specifics. It also leads us to appreciate that we act before and after the questioning, inside and outside the classroom, and with thought as well as action, so to speak — twice the thought, in fact. Here we treat only the first and most crucial phase of teacher questioning, choosing the questions to ask.

The principle of practice is *to discipline behavior in service of purpose in circumstance*. That gives us three things to take into account as we choose our questions: pedagogical purposes, classroom circumstances, and questioning behaviors. An informed choice selects and interrelates all three.

Figure 3.1 conveniently displays these elements of choice. You might use Figure 3.1 by pencilling in details of your case, and by drawing lines to trace the interrelations among purposes, circumstances, and behaviors.

Figure 3.1: Questioning to purpose

Pedagogical Purposes

– why?

   to what end?

+

Classroom Circumstances

1. *Learner* – who?

2. *Subject-matter* – what?

3. *Activity* – how?

4. *Milieu* – where & when?

5. *Result* – who learns what?

↑

Questioning Behaviors

1. *Usage* – whether to question?

2. *Quantity* – how many questions?

3. *Kind* – what type of question?

4. *Topic* – about what?

5. *Form* – in which terms?

6. *Addressee* – to whom?

7. *Timing* – when? for how long?

8. *Manner* – in which manner?

9. *Presumptions* – with which beliefs
    & expectations?

10. *Purpose* – what for?

Pedagogical purposes

The choice of questions begins by determining our purposes. Consider that teaching is something of a deliberate, intentional activity. It is purposive action. For at least some of the actions that we perform as teachers, we have purposes in mind. Our purposes are the first thing we have to take into account in the use of questions. And we must first know what our purposes are.

The generic question of purpose is *Why?* or *To what end?* The answer tells nothing about teacher questions; it tells us about our purposes. But as we happen to be examining our purposes as part of the act of using questions, we ask: What am I using questions *for*?

The generic purpose of teaching is that students learn that which is being taught to them through this act of teaching. So we might say that we are using questions for learning. Unfortunately that tells us next to nothing. It might inspire our effort but it does not inform our practice. It says nothing practical about *this* act of teaching and *that* use of questioning.

Teachers may have a hundred purposes for their action. One teacher may have any of a dozen purposes for any single act, such as the act of using a question. Another teacher may have different purposes for the same act. In other words, purposes are particular. You are the appropriate one to answer the question of purpose: What am I using questions *for*?

You soon discover that you have purposes of different kinds, not just different purposes. For example, you have an immediate purpose in this moment for this act of questioning; you have an intermediate purpose for today's questions; and you have an ultimate purpose for using questions in this class or course. The actions all seem part of some whole, as if this act of questioning formed an integral part of today's use of questioning and the overall use of questioning in the course. But they are not. They are different actions with distinct purposes. More often than not, these purposes are dissimilar and even discordant.

That makes it silly for us to think that questions have a purpose — this purpose or that purpose. It is we who have the purposes, several purposes of different kinds; and it is we who use questions to serve those purposes. Hence it is wise for us to know our purposes from the start, and to use questions this way and that for this and that purpose.

In the meantime we wisely bear in mind that the questions might not prove to serve our purpose. We will not know that until after the asking. For the moment all we are doing is discovering our purposes and fitting the use of questions. Other circumstance now enter into our choice of questions, complicating the fit.

Classroom circumstances

We do not hold purposes all by themselves, as it were, but in circumstances of action. And we do not use questions in isolation, as if to befit purpose alone, but to suit purpose in circumstance. Now we have to consider our classroom circumstances and the purposes we hold in them. Again it is a matter of particulars. That makes for a more and more particular choice. You as the teacher are the one to make the choice.

The classroom may be a single place but it is a complex of multiple contexts. Classroom circumstances vary, within one and the same classroom and during the very same lesson. The teacher faces a hundred circumstances. These conspire with his hundred purposes. You will have to connect purposes and circumstances in order to choose the appropriate questioning behaviors.

You can master this situation by understanding the *kinds* of things involved. Consider that teaching consists of teacher and learner interacting over subject-matter in circumstance towards an intended result. We are already considering the teacher and purposes. Now we see what else is involved — the learner, the subject-matter, the activity, the milieu, and the result (Figure 3.1).

Purposes attach to each of these, and not to each alone but to each in relation to the others. For instance, my purpose for teaching includes a purpose for teaching this subject-matter, and further includes a purpose for teaching this subject-matter to these students, and here and now. As purposes and circumstances vary, so does the questioning.

To illustrate, here is a particularly vivid example which you, the reader, can now supply. Picture yourself teaching in a classroom. Please fill in the picture by pencilling in some details:

> Today is _____. I am in classroom no. _____ during the _____ period or hour. I am teaching the subject, _____, at the _____ level or grade. Before me in the classroom there are _____ pupils, among whom are named _____, _____, and _____.

With this picture ever in mind, let us review your circumstances.

1. Learner — Who?

The generic question is *Who*? or, whom am I teaching? (Figure 3.1).

The learner is your class of students and the individual student. You have at least two different purposes as you teach the class and the individual; hence you may use questions differently with the class and with this and that individual student — whether you are teaching that student alone or in class. Whether as class or individual, the learner is particular, never generic. Your students are defined by name, age, gender, school level, ethnicity, looks, intelligence, interests, and so forth. You are teaching *these* students. You have purposes for teaching them. For example, you have purposes for acting with the smart or cooperative pupils, and purposes for defiant or dumb ones. You use questions to purpose for the learner.

2. Subject-matter — What?

What am I teaching them?

The subject-matter is the topic at hand in the moment, the lesson for today, the subject of the course, the curriculum for the year. You have purposes for each. Each has cognitive, affective, behavioural aspects — something to know, to feel, to do. Each has characteristics of simplicity and complexity, difficulty and ease, fact and fantasy. You use questions to purposes for these subject-matters as they vary and interrelate with these learners. To appreciate this point, recall to mind the picture of your classroom and work out a few of the combinations of subject-matter and learner. For instance, take the topic at hand in this moment and relate its characteristics to the characteristics of the three pupils you named. Which questions about which aspects of this topic would you ask which students?

3. Activity — How?

How am I going about teaching this subject-matter to these students?

The activity is not the teacher's alone. Students too are acting; teacher and learner interact. The teaching-learning activity in your class at this moment might be recitation or discussion, lecture or other presentation, seatwork and so on; it may be a whole-class activity, small group, or individual. Your purposes for these activities vary, at the same time as varying with the subject-matter and learners involved with you in the activity. So too will your use of questions vary. For instance, the use of questions in recitation and discussion will differ.

4. Milieu — Where and when?

In which conditions am I now teaching this subject to these learners through this activity?

All manner of conditions, from within and without, circumscribe the milieu in your classroom. For instance, one factor is time. Time describes the history and development of this classroom. You do not act today as if no yesterday were circumscribing your action. Hence you do not ask a question out of the blue but in a condition fully informed by previous events and class developments, based on achieved knowledge and developed willingness to answer. For example, you use questions differently with children who have shown reluctance or eagerness to participate, and again with those whose record of eager answers is consistently wrong or right. Time further describes the immediate moment and what has just transpired — such as an answer just given. Which question, to whom, about what, is apt at this moment? Time also describes duration. Is there enough time for questions now? Conversely, does questioning represent the best use of the time available? Or yet, shall time be made for questioning? Finally, time describes the very moment of questioning. How long to wait for an answer from this student on this topic? Hence we use questions differently as conditions of time — and other aspects of milieu — vary with subject-matter, learner, and activity.

5. Result — Who learns what?

As I am teaching, who is learning what from the teaching?

According as results occur the circumstance changes, and with it the purposes. With these the appropriate use of questions changes. Which questioning behaviors are suitable when students have learned as a result of the teaching? For instance, when they seem to have understood the question-answers. Which questions are suitable when these students and not those have learned this and not that? The enduring problem is that, although results surely occur and circumstances change, these elude our sure detection and firm grasp. Nonetheless we have continually to estimate who is learning what, and moreover as a result of what, in order to continue teaching — and to continue using questions appropriate to purposes in these circumstances.

Questions themselves can be used in order to determine the results in learning, as when we put questions in order to find out the child's understanding of what we have just taught. Yet not any question asked in any manner will reveal to us the mind of this child. To serve that purpose too we will still have, as ever, to discipline our questioning behavior.

Questioning behaviours

The hard part is over. You have taken into account the purposes that you hold in the circumstances you face. Now all you have to do is to choose the appropriate questioning behavior.

It is a complex and detailed matter that we have described to this point. But it is harder to describe than to do. It can be done in a trice. Indeed, teachers must do it in the very moment of classroom action, continually sensing the circumstances and adjusting their moves. You too will do that, as indeed you must. And like other teachers, you will do it more and less well. You can also discipline yourself to spend quiet time before class in long preparation of the questions, choosing the behaviors that serve to purpose in circumstance.

There are hundreds of questioning behaviors to choose from. To inform our choice, let us display for our understanding some of the aspects of questioning behavior (Figure 3.1, p. 54). This is not a list of techniques but ten categories that together constitute the behavior of questioning. Each aspect in each category is open for our choice. We may rightly choose one way or another of enacting each of these aspects. Each way has disadvantages and advantages. Any one way serves to some purposes and not to others, in some circumstances and not others.

To specify our choice among questioning behaviors, we answer the generic question identified for each. That gives the specifics needed for practice.

1. Usage — whether to question?

That is the first choice to make, according as we judge that using questions in this circumstance promises to serve our purposes. We may make the choice for a whole lesson, a given activity, a particular juncture of talk, or yet for some individual student. If we judge that questions are not suitable in this case, many alternatives for interaction are available (see Chapter 5).

2. Quantity — how many questions?

A given number of questions is suitable or not (too many, too few). We can determine the number in consideration of the classroom process, preparing, for example, ten questions for a recitation or one for discussion. Or in consideration of our students, we might prepare one question for each student, to serve the purpose of attending to everyone and making everyone attend. How many questions are sufficient for this seatwork exercise, homework assignment, examination? and so forth.

3. Kind — what type of question?

Questions can be classified into any number of types, and suitable types chosen — closed and open questions, factual and opinion, 'lower' and 'higher' cognitive questions. There are suitable uses for each type in various classroom processes, or for various students, and so forth. No one type is to be used, and no other not used; all types can be useful or not, according to purpose in circumstance.

4. Topic — about what?

Which topics are suitable to ask about in the recitation, for example, or of this child? Given our sense of what students understand, we might ask them about related topics or ask this one about that topic and another student about another.

5. Form — in which terms?

Form describes the choice of words and their arrangement in the question-sentence. All wordings and arrangements constrain or in some way affect the possible answer. For example, a question structured as 'Is X?' (Does? Can? etc.) permits a yes/no answer. A question that specifies alternatives, such as 'X or Y?' ('X, Y, or Z?' etc.) permits one of the specified alternatives to be chosen in answer. Everything then depends on the number and kind of alternatives specified. Questions that begin with the 'wh-' words (and their variants, e.g., 'to what extent?') permit other kinds of answer. Any question can be structured in any of these three ways, and of course filled in with the choice of words. Various choices of vocabulary and structure can be useful or not to various purposes, according to the answers or kind of answer judged desirable.

6. Addressee — to whom?

Questions can be addressed to the whole class or to a selected individual. Purposes and circumstances might require posing questions to some students but not to others, or to all students, or yet certain questions to certain students — for example, bright and dull pupils.

7. Timing — when? for how long?

Questions might be useful or not at any time, or over a certain time; at junctures of activity or talk. A lesson might begin and/or continue and/or end with questions. A specific point of talk, as when a student has just said something, may or may not be a time to pose a question. Timing also entails the sequence of questions and the pace or rate of questioning. Shall a follow-up question be asked? In what place in the sequence? How fast/slow to pose questions, and to speak a given question? How long to wait for an answer to start, and how long for it to finish? At times we should wait and not, for shorter and longer moments.

8. Manner — in which manner?

Manner involves the tone and attitude conveyed, the voice, diction, inflection and other aspects of delivery, as well as the non-verbal aspects such as proximity to respondent, facial gestures, and the like. A smooth conversational manner may be useful, or loud and clear may be called for. The teacher may gaze relaxedly about the room or stare intently at a given student.

9. Presumptions — with which beliefs and expectations?

Certain presumptions might be useful to questions in recitation but not discussion, for example, or for asking this student but not another about this or that topic.

10. Purpose — what for?

This is the purpose we attach to the very question, in addition to our purposes for using questions generally, and our purposes for teaching. What is the purpose for asking this question? Our generic purpose may be to get an answer from the student asked. This purpose is easily frustrated by certain specifics of other aspects of our questioning behavior — particulars of manner and timing; asking a second question just after the first, or even supplying the answer ourselves; and so on. In general, it only makes sense to behave throughout in such a way as to serve the purpose of posing the question in the first place, so that the use of questions will in turn serve educative purposes in classroom circumstance.

Let us recall to mind what is at issue here. All that we are doing is displaying the elements involved in our choosing questions to purpose. We are displaying them for our understanding, so that, for instance, we will know the ten aspects of questioning behavior rather than the thousand and one details of each aspect. A good way to know these is to keep in mind the ten generic questions. By answering these generic questions we choose the specific questioning behaviors suitable to our purposes and circumstances.

That is our first act in using teacher questions. Next we go on to enact our choice in the classroom. Then we reflect on the consequences of enacted choice. This scheme of action yields the pedagogy of teacher questions.

PEDAGOGY OF TEACHER QUESTIONS

Pedagogy enjoins us to take disciplined action before, during and after posing questions. Preparation begins the action and reflection completes it. At each step any number of specific acts are involved, all of them comprehended in the generic scheme of pedagogy to be outlined here (see Figure 3.2).

The generic scheme identifies the *kinds* of acts involved in the action of using teacher questions. In its character as *generic*, the scheme lacks all specifics, particulars, details. And, as generic, it applies to the whole action of teacher questions.

The scheme outlines the acts involved in using teacher questions whatever the classroom process — recitation, discussion, examination, student exercises. Each process, naturally enough, also entails a more specific, less generic pedagogy appropriate to that process, as articulated in the next chapters on recitation and discussion. Finally, each use of questions in any one process further entails quite specific acts, suited to particulars of purpose and circumstance. None of these specifics appears in this scheme. They appear in classroom practice. But the scheme does give the teacher a practical way to derive the specifics for using questions in practice.

The way to derive specifics for practice is to answer the generic question that is attached to each count of action identified in the scheme. The scheme outlines the categories of action together with the question that is answered in the doing of it. By answering the questions each teacher discovers the suitably specific way to enact the kinds of acts that together constitute the use of teacher questions. The alternative is to list out hundreds of questioning techniques for every conceivable purpose and circumstance, appending the dozen exceptions and even contrary recommendations for each case. That is no scheme, and applying it is not pedagogy.

This scheme for teacher questions empowers us to take action by preparing, posing, and pondering questions. The action consists of our *enacted answers* to seven generic questions, one each for the seven counts of action entailed in using teacher questions.

1. What are the questions *for*?
2. How to prepare them?
3. How to pose the question?
4. Who is to answer?
5. What to do with the answer?
6. How did the questions work?
7. Which next questions will work better?

These questions, and others we might prefer to entertain, are answered in action. They may be answered one at a time, step by step, and all at once. A teacher can face all of the questions even before entering the classroom, anticipating the answers — as you the reader will do here, and as you might do in advance planning of a lesson. A teacher can also answer the first two questions at home of an eve, the next three in the classroom on the morrow, and the last two that night — stretching the action out, as it were. A teacher will also answer all of the questions in a trice during the classroom exchange — thinking a moment before and after the moment of posing a question. The duration of the action does not matter. The principle is that all of these acts are involved in using teacher questions. They will be done willy-nilly, whenever they are done and however well.

In presenting the scheme of action here we will take it one step at a time. It will appear as if the teacher were spending some long time in preparing the questions, then entering the classroom to pose them, and later reflecting on the questions with leisure. That is a good impression to have of the schedule of action for teacher questions. But the very same schedule must *in addition* be hurried through in the heat of the classroom exchange. That is a necessity of practical action in such an enterprise as education (and certain others).

Better to discipline ourselves to face the pedagogical questions *also* over a protracted time than to abandon our teaching solely to the devices of the moment. The first thing to do is to prepare the questions long before they are asked.

Figure 3.2: Pedagogy of teacher questions

```
Prepare the Questions
    1. Purpose — what are the questions for?
    2. Preparation — how to ready them for the asking?

Pose the Questions
    3. Question — how to pose the question?
    4. Answer — who is to answer?
    5. Reaction — what to do with the answer?

Reflect on Questions
    6. Assessment — how did the questions work?
    7. Redesign — which next questions will work better?
```

Prepare the questions

Before stepping into the classroom, and in the moment before posing a question, we govern our step in face of two practical issues: What are the questions being used for? How to ready them for good use? We answer these in action by preparing the questions to purpose.

1. Purposes — what are the questions for?

At issue are our purposes for using questions in the first place. These in turn are formed by the purposes that we hold in the particular circumstances of our teaching.

The first act of using questions is to summon our purposes, making them plainly known to ourselves. Then we can proceed to prepare questions that promise to serve these purposes and not some others.

There is no end to the purposes that questions can serve. Different speakers can hold diverse purposes for asking the same question, and one speaker can hold different purposes for the various questions that he asks. Not all purposes are educative ones, and not all questions serve educative purposes — including the purposes and questions of teachers.

One generic purpose for asking questions is to obtain answers in return. (There are other generic purposes too; a question may be asked for this purpose *plus* another; and many questions are asked *not* for this purpose at all, even when answers are given.) Using the notion of answers helps us to discover our purposes for asking; and it helps again to devise particular questions that will serve these purposes, via the answers.

The question of purpose can be answered by discovering our intents with respect to answers. The question assumes this form: *What do I want the answer for?* Related general questions include:

- What is it that I want to know or to find out?
- What kind of answer do I want?
- How will that answer work to tell or to show me what I intend it to?
- What will I do with the answer?

Asking these questions raises to mind in a clear and pointed way our purposes for using questions, then clearly points our way towards the particular questions to prepare.

2. *Preparation — how to ready the questions for the asking?*

The issue here is not whether the question shall be prepared. It is a practical blunder to pose questions that have not been prepared specifically for the asking, and in specified circumstances of practice.

Pedagogy enjoins experienced and inexperienced teachers to prepare questions before asking them and to ask questions that have been prepared. It is a practical matter. Without it there are just a lot of questions being asked, but little skill to the questioning and little service to educative purpose.

At issue are the actions to take beforehand in fitting the questions to purpose and suiting them to be posed. All the detailed things that may be in need of doing will come to light as we write, arrange, and rehearse the questions. A useful guide at each step is the notion of answers.

Write the questions. Literally write the questions down on a piece of paper, forming each one word for word and continually reforming it until satisfied that it expresses the question that you have in mind. Then sketch the various possible answers permitted by this form of the question, collecting all the answers that you can imagine and anticipate. Reformulate the question until it permits the answers or kind of answers that you judge desirable or correct and so on. That is to model the question after a model of the answer.

Arrange the questions. Arrange the questions in an order that you judge suitable. Use any principle of ordering and any mode of displaying the order on paper. Several arrangements are yielded by tracing the interrelations among the answers you have sketched. Knowing these interrelations beforehand will permit you to ask the appropriate next question in class, whatever the prepared order, according to the answer that is actually given.

Rehearse the questions. Speak the questions aloud to yourself in a classroom voice and manner. (Reading and whispering will not do.) Clear away the correct answer by first speaking it in your mind, next speak the question aloud and then one or two novel, alternative answers to the question *as spoken.* That will let you hear the sound and sense that the questions make to your ear; and it will yield new answers (correct or not) that are useful for revising the question or completing the set of answers. Finally, hold a dress rehearsal by putting the questions to a collaborator, seeing how someone else makes sense of the question and actually answers it. Use this question-answer to touch up your final preparations. Now the questions are ready for asking and answering on the classroom stage.

Pose the questions

On the stage of classroom action we pose the questions that we have carefully prepared for the asking. Again we discipline our behavior so that the act of posing the questions serves to purpose in this circumstance.

As we proceed, other questions too come to mind and appear good to ask in the moment. The same principle applies, and the same pedagogy. These spontaneous questions too must be prepared and posed to purpose in circumstance. Hence we do not ask questions on the spur of the moment or off the cuff, as they happen to pop into our mind and roll off our tongue. Rather we give a moment's thought to the question. We hesitate to ask, as it were, taking a second to examine and formulate it. Then on second thought we ask the question or not. Without this discipline we will likely be asking everyday questions, not educative ones. Better not to ask questions on the spur of the moment but only on second thought.

Posing a question turns out to entail not one but three moves — asking, answering, reacting. To decide the specific way of enacting each move, we can answer the generic question identified here for each. We answer in action. These are the practical answers which only you can give.

3. Question — how is the question to be posed?

We have already prepared the question; at issue is the manner of posing it. The particulars of manner describe tone, pace, attitude, and the like.

In general, we do well to ask *with interest in the answer*. Our manner of asking will display our interest, whatever it is. We express interest in the answer whether we know the answer or not, by asking as if the answer were a matter of some interest to us. And indeed it is, for it is in the interest of answers that we pose questions.

When asking a perplexed question, we should do so with open interest in the answer that we do not have, revealing rather than veiling our interest, and appealing for the needed help — whether information in direct answer or joint effort to construct an answer. By contrast, the everyday strategy is to express some question other than the one that perplexes, and then quietly to use the answer, by deduction, to satisfy secret interests. This is common in the dating game. For an innocent example, 'What are you doing Saturday night?' It is not uncommon in academic settings either. In the first class session of a new term students regularly ask me, 'Can you tell us a little bit about your background?' The question turns out to be either 'Are you married?' or 'Where did you go to college?' At a seminar for researchers one participant asked: 'Would you go through this outline with us point for point before we go on?' (I would not.) The question turned out to be: 'What does the word "nomothetic" mean on line 36 of the second page?' (asked privately afterwards). It is difficult, perhaps socially irregular, to ask in a manner that reveals our interest in the answer. That is just the manner to use regularly in the classroom.

When posing the question for discussion, whether it perplexes us or not, we do so with interest in the several answers that the discussion process will yield. We might write the question on the board, presenting it as an issue in the student discussion of which we are plainly interested. Here we express interest in the process of answering as well as in the answers.

When putting questions during a recitation, when assigning questions for seatwork or homework, and when setting questions for examination, we plainly are not interested in the answer that we already know. Rather we pose them with a pointed interest in the answer that the student will give. Otherwise the asking is lifeless, as the answering will surely be.

Our proper interest is not in the production of the correct answer but in the answer that the student produces. The first interest is satisfied when, during a recitation for example, any student gives the answer that is correct, whether or not he answers knowingly, and whether or not any other students can give and know the correct answer. The second interest is satisfied when this student and then that student gives the answer that he and she knows, whether it is correct or incorrect.

To pose questions without interest in the answer serves several purposes, but few educative ones. For instance, we will not find out what the students know and how they know it. Aptly sensing our disinterest in their answers and our interest only in the production of the correct answer, students will conduct themselves in ways that satisfy the interest of the asking. They will arrange for the production of the correct answer. During a recitation they will designate a few able and eager classmates to give the right answers; they will not volunteer their answer; when called on they will guess at the right answer or parrot it rather than foolishly give the answer in their mind. On study assignments they will mindlessly scour materials for that item which is the correct answer, and vacuously fill the blank. Or they will beg, borrow, buy, and steal answers to homework and examination questions. All of these ways assure the production of the correct answers. It is then on this production, one not of the students' mind, that the teacher bases his sense of the student's mind and his choice of the next appropriate act of teaching. The next questions appear and the production moves ahead.

To ask without interest in the answer is contrary pedagogy. It frustrates the very use of questions, and with it most purposes of teaching and learning.

4. Answer — who is to answer?

Although answering is a student move, teacher action is entailed from the start. As a rule, students cannot speak until so designated by the teacher. At issue here are the particulars of the student both as addressee and as respondent: who to ask, and who to have answer.

The particulars combine student characteristics on the one hand and, on the other, aspects of the teacher's action in designating the student.

The teacher's action allocates, among other things, opportunity to respond, time for response, encouragement and other help in responding. For instance, if the teacher does not give a certain student the opportunity to respond, that student will not give a response. Opportunity can be given in various ways; for example, by putting a question to that student, by calling on that student, or by recognizing that student's bid to respond (e.g., raised hand). These may or may not be the way to give opportunity to a given student in given circumstances and purposes.

As a result, whether intended or not, of the teacher's action, students with specified characteristics become the ones to answer the question. For instance, opportunity to respond will be given either to all, some or one of the students. The main characteristics of the student as candidate for respondent include personal identity or name, gender, seating, race, ethnicity, academic ability, social and linguistic competence, personal comeliness, and willingness to volunteer or to participate. On each of these counts pedagogy enjoins us to discipline our behavior in designating students as respondents.

For each type of student characteristic, the issues for action are:

(a) Which students shall be given the *opportunity* to answer? How to give that opportunity?

(b) Which students shall be given *time* to answer? How much time, for which students?

(c) Which students shall be given *encouragement* and *help* to answer? In what way, for whom?

In addressing each issue, we work out 'which students' according to the various characteristics just specified. For instance, how shall we allocate opportunity, time and help to students who are academically able and less able; fluent and hesitant in speech; seated at center and offsides; volunteering and not volunteering to answer; and so forth.

These are practical matters open for resolution. They can be resolved only by acting in the particular circumstance to suit particular purpose. The apt resolution is not obvious and cannot be determined apart from particulars of practice.

But the generic question can be answered in part. Who is to answer? — in general, *all students are to answer*; and *each student is to give his answer*. That follows from the fact that we are teaching, as a rule, all the students in the room; and we need to know the mind of the student in order to teach him accordingly. In the ideal, all students may not be asked a question but all will be given the opportunity, time, encouragement, and help in answering. How to do that in each case remains an open question to answer in practice.

5. Reaction — what is to be done with the answer?

At issue is the appropriate way to act upon the answer once it has been given.

Ultimately the reaction will be a next instructional act based on the answer — for instance, a next question or next lesson. That will require the intermediate step of evaluating the answer — determining its aptness or correctness, and appreciating what it reveals about the student's knowledge and understanding of the subject matter in question. In turn, there are still prior things to do in the immediate moment.

The first act is to *listen to the answer*. Oddly enough, we cannot take this elementary and obvious step without disciplining our behavior. Otherwise we only half-listen, if at all. For instance, we might be thinking of the next question to ask or be formulating objections or counterexamples. We might even complete in our own minds the other half of the answer that we are not listening to, especially when we have some official or anticipated answer in mind. The boy next to me in Latin class regularly succeeded in giving correct answers that he did not know and did not even speak, by a device that took advantage of the teacher's semi-attention. The wonder of it was that he would give the *second* half of the answer, while the teacher filled in the first. Time and again McD. would pass his finger across his lips while murmuring nonsense, then withdraw them to enunciate '*-are, -avi, -atus*'. 'Good!' the teacher would say, then he would supply the first half and repeat the second, adding, 'That's right'. (The first half is the unknown, and the only variant in the formula; the second half is the typical sequence for hundreds of verb-stems.)

As a result of not listening we might miss the answer or some part of it, together with its character, and pass up the opportunity of discovering the student's state of mind. Listening gives us the information we need to judge the kind of answer that the student gives, and whether it is in fact an answer that he is giving.

Answers can be correct or incorrect, acceptable or impermissible, partial or complete, direct or indirect, expected or unanticipated, and combinations of these. An answer can be correct on various grounds without being the correct answer that we have in mind. For instance, it may correctly answer the question as asked but not the question we mean to ask. Partial and direct answers, when correct, may permit us to infer that the student knows by implication the complete and direct answer; we can then check our inference. Several answers may be acceptable other than the one we have in mind, and none or all of them may be correct. For instance, the question may permit divergent answers, none of them to be preferred as correct; or alternative formulations of the answer, all of them correct. Not every divergent answer or alternative formulation is acceptable, however, even when correctness of answer is not at issue. With the official answer in mind, we may tend not to listen to the answer that is being given.

In any of these cases, a useful reaction is to identify for the student the kind that we judge the answer to be, then let the student respond further. For instance, the student might complete a partial answer, explain an unanticipated answer, straighten out an indirect answer, and justify both a correct and an incorrect answer. Any type of answer deserves further comment by the student. Other students might also comment in reaction.

Listening helps determine whether it is an answer to begin with. Students are to give answers, but all manner of non-answer responses can tolerably be given to a question. The teacher has to know what is going on and react accordingly.

Consider, for example, the response 'I don't know.' That is a good answer, when literally correct. It may otherwise mean that the student does not know what to say; that he is forming an answer to give in the next moment; that he has an answer but does not know if it is correct, or whether to venture it. He may have an answer that corrects the question and thus the teacher. He may have no answer or none to give. He may have an answer, a correct answer, know it to be correct but refuse to give it. He may be unwilling to speak at all. Safer to say 'I don't know' than 'I refuse to answer', or 'I'm embarrassed/reticent/inattentive', etc.

Or the student may joke and make other cute replies, request that the question be repeated, shrug, and the like. Another strategy is to speak so painfully slowly, starting and restarting a sentence with non-informative words and then pausing to the point where the teacher calls upon someone else.

In all of these cases of non-answer responses, the teacher has to weigh the character of the response, the meaning of the words, the cause or source, and the educative significance of it all. Does it signify an academic matter calling for instruction, or a social matter calling for management? Perhaps it calls for nothing at all but prudently to leave matters alone and move on. Whatever the case, the teacher must react deftly.

Good humor disposes us to appreciate the comedy of our question-answer at times, when we and the students take literally the odd questions we are putting to them. ('How many sheep did the farmer have in the other pasture?' and the like.) On examination papers students sometimes write both a literal and a safely correct answer to our questions, or annotate them with cartoons, doodles, venturesome comments and other traces of actuality. There is the old story about an oral examination in university physics or mathematics. 'Using only a barometer, how can you find the height of a building?' The candidate gave several successive replies, none of them mathematical but all literally correct, culminating with this one: 'Take the barometer to the building's manager or owner and give it to him in exchange for telling you the height of the building.' What is the appropriate teacher reaction to that plainly incorrect answer? What use can be made of it to weigh the student's knowledge of mathematics? — the matter in question. Which question or manner of putting it would serve better to that purpose?

Reflect on questions

Reflection completes the action of using questions. Having just posed the question that we had earlier prepared for the asking, we now act to reflect on our enacted choices and their consequences.

Reflection follows the act of asking, both immediately and subsequently. Immediately upon posing the question we reflect on it, in the very heat of classroom action. Subsequent to posing all the questions we reflect on them, at a calm remove from the classroom (e.g., at home). Reflection completes the action whether the action lasts for a moment or for an hour.

The reflective act answers two questions: How did the question work? Which next questions will work better? That determines the consequences of our enacted choice.

6. *Assessment — how did the questions work?*

At issue are the characteristics of the questions that we actually posed, and their functions in the teaching-learning process. In order to assess the functions we first assess the characteristics.

System is required for finding out the actual events of questioning (asking, answering, reacting) in the classroom. Recollections and estimates do not serve this purpose. To our surprise we learn that teachers are not competent to report with *any* accuracy the questioning that occurs in their classroom. Their estimates are wildly off. No matter. When asking questions we are doing vital other things, not maintaining clerical records. We will therefore set up a system to do the recording for us. Then we can reflect on the record.

The system has to be established before the fact. We need to devise a systematic way of capturing something of the questioning events, *and* we had best decide beforehand those events that are to be captured.

We can choose to use a number of systematic devices. All are useful, each in a different way or to a different purpose. For instance, they capture different events of questioning or different aspects of the same event.

• *Tape-recording*, audio- and/or visual. Record both the teacher and the students, and record both of them during the asking and the answering.

• *Stenography*. Engage selected students or a colleague to tally and/or to transcribe the desired events or aspects of questioning.

• *Memo*. On your own list of questions prepared for the lesson, jot, circle, mark, and annotate during class. In the last moments write a memo or set of notes as if for someone else, not another teacher but a visitor from Mars. (People from Mars need the obvious explained.)

• *Interview and questionnaire*. Ask students to report on selected items of interest which they are competent to evidence (e.g., their unspoken thoughts, their reactions to question-answer exchanges witnessed). Sort the evidence by selected characteristics of the students (e.g., seating, academic ability, whether they answered in class).

That will yield a record. Now we examine the record for the questions and their functions.

Some of the matters to examine will already have been identified or otherwise defined by the nature of the recording system and the kind of record it can make. For other matters we prepare an itemized list to check off as we examine the record. For instance, we can listen to a tape-recording with a form in front of us to guide our listening. The form specifies the assessment questions that we are asking about our classroom questions.

Several useful forms are at hand for our ready use. These are full of informative questions to ask about our classroom questions.

• *The list of questions we prepare for the class*. Compare the prepared and the posed questions.

• *The list of questioning behaviors in Figure 3.1 (p. 54)*. Look for all or any of the ten listed behaviors, each with a question attached as guide to looking, in one or all of your classroom questions.

• *The scheme for posing questions*, in the previous paragraphs. Examine the record for #3-4-5, question-answer-reaction, each with a question attached as guide.

As we assess the characteristics of our questions, reflection already is proceeding over their functions. There are innumerable details of interest. The broader questions run:

- How well did the questions function as a *teaching* device?
- In what way did they service the *classroom* process at hand (e.g., recitation, discussion)?
- To what extent, in which respect, and for whom, did the questions facilitate the process of *learning* (e.g., students' thinking and speaking)?

The generic question runs: *How did the questions serve educative purposes in these classroom circumstances*? In answer we take our classroom questions — and most especially the answers — to Figure 3.1, tracing their way through the particulars of purpose and circumstance. Then we will know how the questions worked.

7. Redesign — which next questions will work better?

At issue is a new design on action, renewing the activity of teacher questioning.

Having revealed to us how our questions worked, reflection moves us to ponder the questions to ask next. But it has also revealed how we understand questions. Reflection thus moves us to study before making a new design.

We study those matters about questioning that we need to understand. This is the understanding needed to inform practice. That gives us the guide to study, the points to learn. As aids to study and learning we have the other chapters in this book; the readings and exercises at the end of the chapters; the people and activities in this course; the record of our own classroom questioning; and the proceedings in other classes we observe, including the transcripts in the Appendix. We use these aids to learn those things about questioning that we have noted but do not understand. For instance, we might not understand how it happens that certain answers are given to our questions. By perusing a book on logic or linguistics about question-answer relations, we come to understand both the student's answer and our own question, as well as how they may or may not sensibly relate. With that understanding we inform our practice.

Our new design on action addresses 'which questions' to use next. That is a generic issue. It leads us to reflect on the use of *student* questions as well as teacher questions, on the *questions* to use in each case, and on other *uses* of questions. One other use is to teach students about questions and answers in general, and in particular how to use them in learning as well as how we use them in teaching.

All of that is to use our understanding of questions, gained from reflective practice, to inform our further practice. With that practical understanding the pedagogy of teacher questions is complete.

The scheme of action begins with preparing the questions, continues through posing the questions and ends in reflecting on questions.

The first acts are to identify the purpose for using questions and to form particular questions suited to purpose, readying them for good use by writing, arranging, and rehearsing the questions.

The next acts are to pose the questions in class, going on to choose the respondent and to react to the response by listening and evaluating the answer.

The final acts are to assess the workings of the questions used and to design the next use of questions to enhance teaching and learning.

That is to discipline pedagogical behavior in service of educative purposes in classroom circumstances.

The pedagogy of teacher questions finds complement in the pedagogy of student questions, joining in the pursuit of teaching and learning through questioning. The schemes in this and the previous chapter will in the next two chapters be articulated to the use of student and teacher questions during recitation and discussion.

CORRELATED READINGS

A Education

Andre, T. (1987) 'Questions and learning from reading', *Questioning Exchange*, *1*, 47–86 (London: Taylor & Francis) — a review of studies on written questions that are inserted into reading materials as aids to processing, comprehending, and retaining what is read.

Dillon, J.T. (1979) 'Defects of questioning as an interview technique', *Psychology in the Schools*, *16*, 575–580 — a cautionary discussion about the usefulness of questions for counseling and interviewing students.

Dillon, J.T. (1980) 'Curiosity as non-sequitur of Socratic questioning', *Journal of Educational Thought*, *14*, 17–22; Dillon, J.T. (1981) 'The questions and dialogues of Jesus', *Living Light: An Interdisciplinary Review of Christian Education*, *18*, 199–215 — studies of how two famous teachers used questions.

Dillon, J.T. (1982) 'The effect of questions in education and other enterprises', *Journal of Curriculum Studies*, *14*, 127–152 — a critical review of opinions about the effects of teacher questions, by contrast to what is known about questions from research in education and other fields.

Dillon, J.T. (1982) 'Male-female similarities in class participation', *Journal of Educational Research*, *75*, 350–353 — a correlation study and discussion of how apparent difference in boys' and girls' rates of participation in class can be seen as similarities.

Gall, M.D. (1970) 'The use of questions in teaching', *Review of Educational Research*, *40*, 707–721 — a review of the literature on teacher questions before 1970.

Hargie, O. (1984) 'Training teachers in counselling skills', *British Journal of Educational Psychology*, *54*, 214–220 — a study of training teachers to use questions for counseling and guidance of students in ways very different from their use of questions in classroom teaching.

Macmillan, C.J.B. and Garrison, J. (1983) 'An erotetic concept of teaching', *Educational Theory*, *33*, 157–166 — an intriguing notion that 'to teach' is to answer the students' questions, whether or not the questions are posed aloud.

McNamara, D.R. (1981) 'Teaching skill: The question of questioning', *Educational Research*, *23*, 104–109 — a critical inspection of the advice that teacher-education textbooks give about using questions while teaching.

Readence, J. and Moore, D. (1983) 'Why questions? A historical perspective on standardized reading comprehension tests', *Journal of Reading*, *26*, 306–313 — the engaging history of how questions, specifically, and not other devices, came to be used on standardized tests.

Sigel, I.E. and Saunders, R. (1979) 'An inquiry into inquiry: Question asking as an instructional model', in L. Katz (ed.), *Current topics in early childhood education*, Norwood, N.J.: Ablex, 169–193 — a detailed theory on using questions to enhance the thinking and cognitive development of young children.

Winne, P.H. (1979) 'Experiments relating teachers' use of higher cognitive questions to student achievement', *Review of Educational Research*, *49*, 13–50 — a detailed critical review of all available research on that topic, concluding that the research is inconclusive.

B Other fields

Bolc, L. (ed.) (1980) *Natural language question answering systems*, Munich: Hanser — the detailed theoretical and practical workings of four computerized systems that answer questions put to them in ordinary language.

Bolinger, D.L. (1957) *Interrogative structures of American English*, University, AL: University of Alabama Press; Chisholm, W. (ed.) (1984) *Interrogativity*, Amsterdam: Benjamins — a standard linguistic account of questions in English; and authoritative descriptions of the amazing ways of questions in seven other languages.

Churchill, L. (1978) *Questioning strategies in sociolinguistics*, Rowley, MA: Newbury; Stenstroem, A.-B. (1984) *Questions and responses in English conversation*, Malmoe, Sweden: Gleerup — detailed sociolinguistic studies of how people ask and answer questions, and react to answers, in actual everyday conversations.

Dillon, J.T. (1982) 'The multidisciplinary study of questioning', *Journal of*

Educational Psychology, *74*, 147–165 — a conceptual framework for putting together a comprehensive understanding of questions from what is known about questions in many fields.

Dillon, J.T. (1986) 'Questioning', in O. Hargie (ed.), *A handbook of communication skills*, London: Croom Helm, 95–127 — a detailed description of the elements of using questions skillfully as a communicative device, whatever the context of practice.

Dillon, J.T. (1987) 'The multidisciplinary world of questioning', in W. Wilen (ed.), *Questions, questioning techniques and effective teaching*, Washington, D.C.: National Education Association — a quick tour of the world of questioning, visiting a dozen realms of theory and a dozen realms of practice to see what else is out there beyond education, and what lessons might be brought home to education for the good use of questions.

Harrah, D. (1982) 'What should we teach about questions?' *Synthese*, *51*, 21–38 — a world authority on the logic of questions and rational communication outlines the things about questions that we should teach our students.

Hiz, H. (ed.) (1978) *Questions*, Dordrecht, Holland: Reidel; Kiefer, F. (ed.) (1983) *Questions and answers*, Dordrecht, Holland: Reidel; Meyer, M. (ed.) (1987) *Questions and questioning: An interdisciplinary reader*, Berlin: De Gruyter — anthologies with chapters on various aspects of questioning as seen from the perspectives of several different disciplines, especially logic and philosophy, linguistics and computer science.

Long, L., Paradise, L. and Long, T. (1981) *Questioning: Skills for the helping process*, Monterey, CA: Brooks Cole — a manual on using questions in counseling and psychotherapy.

Metzler, K. (1977) *Creative interviewing: The writer's guide to gathering information by asking questions,*, Englewood Cliffs, N.J.: Prentice-Hall — a manual for journalists on how to use questions to get informative or colorful remarks from people.

Payne, S.L. (1951) *The art of asking questions*, Princeton, N.J.: Princeton University Press — all kinds of practical advice for opinion pollsters and market researchers, with many humorous examples, plus a checklist of 100 considerations in formulating a question.

Plato, *Dialogues*: Lysis, Charmides, Laches; and Apology — charming little renderings of how Socrates used questions; and a poignant rendering of why he did so and what was done to him as a result.

PRACTICAL EXERCISES

1. Grasp a questioning behavior

To do this exercise you will need an instance of behavior. Many instances of teacher questioning are transcribed in the Appendix. Take any one question and get a firm hold on it by turning it through the ten aspects of questioning behavior in Figure 3.1 (p. 54), then by running it through the three steps of question-answer-reaction in the pedagogical scheme in this chapter (steps 3,4,5). See how this instance at hand answers to the 13 generic questions, as far as you can determine from the transcripts.

The first two issues are already settled, the choice whether to question or not (but why?) and the quantity of questions — one, in this case. Next, what type of question is it? about what? in which terms? to whom? when? in which manner? with which presumptions? and what for? Then turn to the pedagogical scheme to see how the question was posed, who answered it and how, and what was done with the answer.

Pursue this exercise on all the teacher's questions considered *together* as one longer instance of questioning behavior. Instead of bearing on each single question, get a grasp of the behavior as a whole — the choices made to question or not, how many questions in all, what kind overall, etc. (Figure 3.1). Then get a sense of the question-answer-reaction in this case.

If a few fellow students will join you in this exercise you can apportion the 13 generic questions among yourselves. Then you can combine the results and discuss the case that you have made. Or each of you can do all 13, on the single question and/or on the collection of questions, then compare your grasp of the case. Everyone should bear on the *same instance* of questioning behavior.

2. Prepare questions for teaching

Prepare the questions that are useful for you to teach the subject matter of this chapter (teacher questions) through a series of class-room processes. Rather than exhaust yourself preparing all of the questions, prepare selected questions for all of the activities in the series.

a. Construct a question-answer outline for your *lecture* on this subject, with three main points (question-answers) plus two sub-points for any one main point you like.

b. Prepare three questions for a *recitation* to follow the lecture, as if in a review.

c. Prepare the single question for a *discussion* based on knowledge from the lecture and recitation.

d. Prepare one of the questions for a suitable *seatwork* or *homework* exercise to follow.

e. Prepare three questions for a written *test* or *examination* over the completed lesson (a-d).

3. Reformulate questions

Take any question that you have formulated for Exercise 2 and reformulate it. (If you have not done Exercise 2, take any question from Exercise 1 or any other question that you are familiar with.)

Rearrange the question into various structures: as a yes/no question; as an alternative or multiple-choice question; and as a question with each of the 'wh-' words or their variants (who, what, when, where, how, why).

Now go on to toy with the choice of words in several of the differently-structured forms of the question. Keep the structure, vary the vocabulary; make two wordings with the same arrangement for the one question.

4. Mini-recitation and exam

Join with one fellow student in a practice recitation and/or examination over the subject-matter of this chapter. Each of you, students A and B, prepare three questions (e.g., from Exercise 2 or 3). Both A and B can prepare recitation questions and/or examination questions; or A can prepare the recitation and B the examination.

Student A then poses the oral or written questions to B, and B answers them orally (recitation) or in writing (examination). You agree that B will answer under the constraint of the question as posed, in its precise form. Then A and B freely exchange comments over how the question was intended by A and understood by B; which answers were expected by A, thought of by B, and permitted or required by the terms of the question; and which appropriate reformulations of question and answer are suggested.

Finally, step aside from the artifice of the exercise and remark on the genuine character of your action. You and your fellow student have been conducting and engaging in a recitation that is based on student questions rather than teacher questions. Take a moment to reflect together on the previous chapter. If you like, proceed to consult the details in the next chapter, under the heading 'An Alternative Recitation' (p. 103).

5. Evaluate responses

Faithfully transcribe the next three question-answers that you hear outside of school, as in everyday exchanges. Do not pick and choose and censor the examples but record the first three you come upon; these will be the good examples that you need for this exercise.

Now judge the character of that which you heard to follow upon the question: whether you judge it to be a non-response, a non-answer response, or an answer. For answers only, judge further whether they are direct or indirect, partial or complete, and the like; and whether they were accepted or not.

Fellow students can each do this exercise and then you can all join to estimate the frequency and character of the things that people do when a question is put to them. Maybe none of you will even have found an *answer* in the cases you observed. In pursuit of this exercise, go out again and look only for answers.

6. Withhold answers

The next time that a question is put to you by a peer (friend, colleague, stranger) or by a social superior (boss, leader, host, etc.) do not answer it. Do anything else instead, giving some non-answer response or some non-response. You know how to do these things.

Do not lie, for a lie is an answer, merely a false one. Do not do this exercise with a social subordinate (child, employee, supplicant), for you never have to answer those questions. Do not do it in a classroom, for you always have to answer those questions.

Note the way in which you managed not to answer, and record your inner and interpersonal experience with not answering. Compare notes with fellow students who in other situations also found ways not to answer.

7. Find the best way to ask

Think up a technique that makes sense to you for asking teacher questions — some appropriate type of question to ask, some good way of asking, any use at all that attracts you. Propound the technique to this chapter, refuting its proposition: *No specifiable technique can rightly be recommended for teacher questioning*. Walk your technique through Figure 3.1, demonstrating for all that it serves to purpose in circumstance.

8. Pose your questions

Identify the questions you have about teacher questions and put them to this chapter. (For details, see the previous chapter's Exercises.)

a. Construe the single question, in your mind, to which this chapter as a whole is an answer.

b. Construct the specific question-answers, in your mind, for main and subordinate sections of the chapter; i.e., make a question-answer outline of it.

c. Restate the questions that, in your expectations at the onset of reading, this chapter would properly be answering or at least addressing. Go on to anticipate the questions for the next chapter.

d. Specify the questions left in your mind after reading the chapter. Bring them to your reading of the remaining chapters, or to other readings about questioning.

9. Track the respondents

You will need to solicit a willing teacher's agreement for you to observe a lesson and to chat with you afterwards. Plainly state only your general motive, such as learning something about classroom processes. Make plain that it is your understanding and not his teaching that is at issue. Do not tell the teacher precisely what you are looking for, as that would unduly influence his behavior (e.g., making him self-conscious or awkward in style).

Quietly but systematically observe the teacher's choice of respondents. Tally the respondents by such characteristics as individual identity, seating arrangement, apparent ability and eagerness to participate, etc. Then chat with the teacher to discover his purposes in these classroom circumstances — learner, subject-matter, activity, milieu, result (Figure 3.1). That will give you what you need to know in order to understand and even to describe the actions you saw. Then you may reflect on the consequences of enacted choice.

10. Reflect on teacher questions

Again you will need a cooperating teacher. Using any system, record any aspect of the use of questions in one class. Again chat with the teacher to discuss purpose in circumstance. Then you can answer the generic question of assessment: *how did the questions work?* And next, redesign: *which use of questions might work better?*

If you can't get into a classroom, you may usefully do this exercise on the transcribed lessons in the Appendix, bearing in mind the limitations of not knowing the teacher's purposes and little about the circumstances.

Whenever you observe a classroom, politely offer to the teacher the record of your observation together with the stated fruits of your understanding. If you and the teacher could then arrange to reflect together on the consequences of enacted choice, you would enjoy a rare event of collegial teaching and learning about the practice of questioning.

4

Questioning and Recitation

OVERVIEW

CHARACTERISTICS OF RECITATION
A characteristic recitation: Mr H's history lesson
Diverse purposes
Distinctive question-answer
  Question
  Answer
  Evaluation

USE OF QUESTIONS AND ANSWERS
Prepare the questions
Ask questions nice and slow
Listen to the answers

AN ALTERNATIVE RECITATION
Preparation
Exchange
Quiz
Evaluation

CORRELATED READINGS

PRACTICAL EXERCISES

Figure 4.1: Pedagogy of recitation questions

Questioning and Recitation

In the broad classroom process described by recitation, the teacher asks questions and the students answer them, reciting what they know or are coming to know of the subject-matter in question. The term is a rubric. Recitation embraces a class of diverse activities and formats all characterized by the same question-answer process. These may otherwise be denoted as oral quiz, review, drill, guided discovery, Socratic method, and the like.

Some of these episodes are elsewhere termed discussion by broad contrast to lecture, referring to the fact that teacher and students are talking back and forth. But all of these episodes are here classed as recitation, by specific contrast to discussion (see Chapter 5), referring to the character of the interaction in the two processes — the manner in which teacher and students talk back and forth, the matter over which they exchange, and the purposes being served.

Recitation is characterized by a distinctive question-answer discourse wherein the teacher asks one question after another, and students give answers in turn. The pace is typically quick and the answers brief, but it can be more leisurely. The distinguishing characteristic of the questions is that what is in question is not what the question asks about. The answers are distinguished as predeterminately correct or incorrect, typically one answer correct for all respondents, as demonstrated by the evaluation that follows upon the answer.

Since recitation is a question-answer process of a kind, everything educational about it turns on the use of questions and answers. The use that is apt in recitation, as elsewhere, serves pedagogical purpose in classroom circumstance. No specific use or technique of questioning can serve the range of purposes and circumstances suitable for recitation. But good general use disciplines the teacher to prepare the questions beforehand, to ask them nice and slow, and to listen to the answers.

An alternative approach bases recitation on student questions. Students as well as teacher prepare questions beforehand. In class, students orally exchange their questions and answers, managing the exchange while the teacher listens and intervenes with instructive comments. Next the teacher contributes a few questions, answered or not. Lastly the questions and answers are evaluated, with the teacher correcting the *questions* and instructing the students on how to use questions for learning. All of that proceeds on the grounds that our knowledge consists in the question-answer propositions that we form of the subject-matter. Whence students recite their knowledge in the form of their questions and answers, in a process of actively asking as well as answering questions.

To see how we might well pursue questioning in recitation, we will first observe the *characteristics of recitation*, illustrating with actual exchanges the various purposes and distinctive features of this question-answer process. Next we consider the good *use of questions and answers*, entertaining practical advice to follow before, during, and after asking questions. Lastly we ponder *an alternative recitation*, working our way through the phases of a practical approach based on student questions as well as answers.

CHARACTERISTICS OF RECITATION

Recitation is an old, recurrent, and familiar event in schoolrooms. One of the oldest and best-known depictions is Plato's dialogue between a slave-boy and Socrates (*Meno*, 82b–85b), wherein by answering Socrates' questions the boy supposedly figures out the hypotenuse of a rectangle. Among the older modern reoccurrences are the numerous dialogues heard by David Page while inspecting elementary schools in 1847 (*Theory and Practice of Teaching*, pp. 81–82), wherein by answering the teacher's questions Charles, for example, figures out the number of sheep in the other pasture. The final eight exchanges will show us how recitations have proceeded through the intervening millennia.

Socrates and boy	*Teacher and Charles*
Here are four squares. Has not each line cut off the inner half of each of them?	Well, Charles, you must first get one-fourth of eight, must you not?
— Yes.	— Yes, sir.
And how many such halves are there in this figure?	Well, one-fourth of eight is two, isn't it?
— Four.	— Yes, sir. One-fourth of eight is two.
And how many in this one?	
— Two.	Well, then, three-fourths will be three times two, won't it?
And what is the relation of four to two?	— Yes, sir.
— Double.	Well, three times two are six, eh?

86

How big is this figure then?
— Eight feet.
On what base?
— This one.
The line which goes from
corner to corner of the square
of four feet?
— Yes.
So it is your personal opinion
that the square on the diagonal
of the original square is double
its area?
— That is so, Socrates.

— Yes, sir.
Very well. Now the book says
that this six is just one-third of
what the farmer had in the
other pasture, doesn't it?
— Yes, sir.
Then if six is one-third, three-
thirds will be — three times
six, won't it?
— Yes, sir.
And three times six are —
eighteen, isn't it?
— Yes, sir.
Then he had eighteen sheep in
the other pasture, had he?
— Yes, sir.

The same sort of thing that Plato wrote and Page heard was stenographically recorded in secondary history and language lessons in 1912 by one of the first researchers on classroom questioning, Romiett Stevens; it was ethnographically recorded in elementary math and social studies lessons in 1981 by Susan Stodolsky; and it has been video-recorded, audio-taped, computer-tracked and chronometrically traced in all manner of other lessons by any number of other researchers in recent years. You can walk into a classroom and see it for yourself. It is all the same thing.

A characteristic recitation

Here is one example of one kind of recitation; it is conducted by Mr H, a pleasant and skilled teacher whose history class has been study-ing the American Revolution. The purpose is to review and to assess what the students know from previous lessons, reading the textbook, and completing special assignments on various aspects of the subject. In this episode the topic in question is the military success of General Washington's revolutionary army. A point has been established about Washington's leadership qualities, and the ques-tions turn to other reasons for success.

   T: OK, so we've kind of covered leadership and some of the
      things that Washington brought with it. Why else did they

win? Leadership is important, that's one.

S: France gave 'em help.

T: OK, so France giving aid is an example of what? France is an example of it, obviously.

S: Aid from allies.

T: Aid from allies, very good. Were there any other allies who gave aid to us?

S: Spain.

T: Spain. Now, when you say aid, can you define that?

S: Help.

T: Define 'help'. Spell it out for me.

S: Assistance.

T: Spell it out for me.

S: They taught the men how to fight the right way.

T: Who taught?

S: The allies.

T: Where? When?

S: In the battlefield.

T: In the battlefield?

(and so on)

This kind of talk is normal enough in classrooms but it still shows several striking features. One feature is that the teacher speaks at every turn at talk. That means that all the other potential speakers, the students, together have every other turn — one turn for all students, taken by some one student speaker. More striking, when the teacher speaks he usually asks a question. Since he speaks at every turn, he is asking a question at every turn. As a result, students speak in answers. That means they do not say anything else, since their every turn at talk follows a question (or a very occasional imperative). They do not talk to anyone else but the teacher; they do not talk about anything else but the teacher's topic; their talk is an answer to the teacher's question, not a comment or question about another matter or to another participant. Moreover, when students speak they speak briefly. That is because they are giving answers when they speak, in turn because the teacher is asking questions when he speaks. And the answers are treated as if they were either correct or incorrect, their correctness being known before the asking and being confirmed after the answering. All of these features are characteristic of recitation.

The pace in Mr H's recitation happens to be fast. The illustrated excerpt lasts little more than half a minute. Mr H asks a question about every five seconds, with student answers lasting about one second. In this style, students have little time to think or to review their understanding or even to display their knowledge. Rapidity of pace is not essential to recitation. The essential factor is that the teacher speaks in questions.

For example, the Appendix illustrates more leisurely recitations conducted by two very experienced teachers (as well as a more extensive excerpt from Mr H's fast recitation). Mr L asks 3–4 questions per minute and student answers last two seconds. Ms HT asks 2–3 questions per minute and the answers last three seconds. It's all the same. In all three recitations, the teacher asks questions at every turn, the students answer briefly in turn, and the answers are rated right or wrong. Students are reciting what they know or are supposed to know in answer to questions. Everything else follows from that.

Diverse purposes

Numerous purposes and circumstances are served by a recitational mode of teaching. It is pointless to specify some one purpose, for purposes and circumstances vary even within a single recitation lesson, not to mention the innumerable purposes that a teacher might have for asking any conceivable question of any student at any juncture. Even at a broad level, some dozen vague purposes are served by recitation.

One broad purpose is to get students to talk, that is to stimulate their responding and class participation, so as to do various things with the talk in response. But teachers may have in mind merely and at least to get the students to talk in the first place. This purpose is easily appreciated by recognizing that a question-mode is just the kind of talk that adults normally engage in with children.

For instance, while walking on campus with my four-year-old son Jay, I met one of my doctoral students and I introduced the two. Here is what he said to Jay, and all that he said:

How old are you?
Do you go to school?
Where?
Do you like it there?
Do you have a sister?
How old is she?

What's her name?
Is this your Daddy?
Is this where your Daddy works?
Do you come here often with him?
Do you think it's pretty here?
Well, I have to go. Nice meeting you, Jay.

Imagine encountering such an interesting person as this man is in a wonderful new world, and then engaging in such a conversation! Of course, most adults are not as polished in their conversational approach to children as is this courteous man and experienced teacher of communication skills at a local college. For instance, I was talking on the phone to my sister when Jay started jumping up and down to have a word with her. That day, despite my best efforts, we had gotten a new puppy dog. Here is what Jay said to his aunt.

We have a new puppy dog!
Rocco.
Brown.
Seven weeks.
Yesterday.
The lady.
Yes.
I don't know.
Yeah . . .
(hands the phone to me and leaves the room)

Imagine just bursting to tell a piece of interesting news to a favorite person about a fascinating development in life, and then engaging in such a conversation!

Of course, we as adults and teachers know that children have little enough of interest to say because they have little enough in their minds and few interesting experiences. The proof is when we try to talk with them. They will hardly even speak, despite our good efforts to join them in conversation, for their discourse seems limited to one- or two-word answers to questions, even to our open, inviting ones.

Where did you go?
— Out.
What did you do?
— Nothing.

What did you learn in school today?

— . . .

With adults, on the other hand, even with friends, we dare not take a question approach lest they sanction us for treating them like children or, worse, like students.

Other broad purposes for recitation include reviewing and assessing what students know from what they have just studied or been taught, as in Mr H's class. 'Did you read anywhere in the book where his army was destroyed?' — 'Those of you who worked on that question about the army — what did you find out about the army itself?'

Another purpose is to get students to think, working out an understanding of what has just been reviewed, as in Ms HT's class (see Appendix). 'Now wait a minute, don't turn to your book. Let's just think something out here. What did those people agree to before they got off the boat?' — 'Yes, but I wish you'd explain "self-government" to me. You know, you're giving me a phrase that I've used over and over, and it's a phrase used in your book. But when you don't put it into the context of a discussion, I don't really know what you're saying.' But the students knew what they were doing when they reached for their books, because Ms HT's class turned out to be a recitation, not a discussion.

Another purpose is to see that students have grasped some particular point of importance to this and future lessons, as in Mr L's class (Appendix). 'Now I would like to make sure you realize how these particular wars were fought. Remember — Why did Braddock lose at DuQuesne?' — 'Do you think England had a right to do this — restrict the colonists, put on the stamp tax? Well, you get into that touchy situation now — did the colonists have a right to revolt? You know, right/wrong. That's a question we'll get into when we get to the Revolutionary War. Was this a right thing to do? Well, in what way do you think England might have been right to do this?' Mr L also uses questions to engage students in his ongoing discourse — to keep their attention, to see if they are following, to complete his sentences, to provide transitions from one point or topic to another, constructing the story through question-answer and frequently checking the foundations and layers.

Still other purposes of recitation are to examine, test, or quiz; to drill, practice, check homework; to introduce, guide, or lead up to new material and points; to probe, challenge, and solidify the knowledge that students are acquiring about the subject-matter in question. It can be any subject-matter, at any level. The questions can be of any type, asked at any pace (but typically fast). For example, the type of questions varies in the illustrated recitations, just as does the frequency and pace of questions.

Mr H asks, among other things, why Washington's army won the war; what made him militarily successful; what difference there is between certain statements; what meaning certain concepts have; what students think Washington's success was, taking everything into account.

Mr L asks why the English won the earlier war against the French; what different reasons the French and English had for emigrating; what the American colonists felt after helping to win that war; and whether England had the right to do what it did to the colonists afterwards, in view of the upcoming question of whether the colonists subsequently had the right to do what they did to England.

Ms HT asks for the reasons behind the Mayflower Compact and for explanations of the later decision to the entire contrary, then for comparisons with present circumstance in the students' own city on the relationship between wealth and political influence: Why did/didn't they? Why do you suppose?

None of this matters. Whatever the purposes and circumstances, whatever the subject-matter and level, whatever the number and pace and kind of questions, the critical factor is that the teacher is asking questions when speaking. In turn the students speak in answers. The answers are treated by teacher and students alike as correct or incorrect, and they are announced and accepted as such. This question-answer is characteristic of recitation.

Distinctive question-answer

Whatever the varieties and particulars, recitation always and everywhere features one and the same distinctive discourse. The whole of this discourse follows from the singular factor of the teacher's questions. That is, the form that recitation takes is a natural consequence of the social and linguistic fact that when the teacher speaks, it is in questions that the teacher is speaking. From that, for example, it follows as a matter of course that students speak in answers. Many other features emerge in tow, all of them dragged in by the questions.

The procedure is as clear as day, and as simple as 1–2–3.

1. The teacher asks a question.
2. A student gives an answer.
3. The teacher evaluates the answer, and in the same breath asks another question.

At every step the speaker and the act are predictable, and the order of steps is invariable. No one else can do anything else. It is as if people were enchained in the discourse. This is the normal course of events precipitated by a teacher question during recitation.

As one side result, the teacher will wind up speaking for about two-thirds or more of the time. (Mr H talks for 69 per cent of the time, Ms HT for 75 per cent and Mr L for 90 per cent.) All of the students together will speak about one-third of the time — but of course, one student at a time, ordinarily, and most students at no time during the lesson. The teacher may speak briefly or expansively, but students will speak briefly. (Mr H speaks for 5 seconds per turn, Ms HT for 10 and Mr L for 20; their students all speak for 3 seconds or less.) That follows naturally from the fact that students are speaking in answer to teacher questions; and having answered as asked, they await the teacher's evaluation plus next question. 1–2–3.

1. Question

The distinctive feature of recitation questions is that what is in question is not the thing that the question asks about, but something else. That is normal enough for questions asked nearly everywhere in our experience: by far the majority of questions are put for some reason and purpose other than the questioner's discovery of the information in answer, even in cases where the questioner does not know the information. In classroom recitations, whatever reason and purpose the teacher might have for asking the question, it is foregone that the matter is not in question for the teacher. Indeed, it is actively presumed that the teacher already knows the answer. Moreover, the student is also supposed to know it or to be quite close to knowing it; it is universally regarded as a violation to presume that the student does *not* know the answer (it is fair to presume either that the student may know or does know the answer). One of the multiple things that may be in question for the teacher is whether or not the student knows the answer or can or will supply it.

The presumptions of the act of questioning in a recitation are that the teacher believes that the presupposition of the question is true and believes further that the student at least does not disbelieve it; the teacher at least does not not-know the answer to the question and does not believe that the student does not know. Teacher and student are invited to share these presumptions. Therefore there are unfair or insincere questions, widely asked by teachers in hopes of making students 'think'.

For example, there are the trick or trap questions that the teacher well knows to have no correct answer because the teacher fully believes that the presupposition to the question is false. (That is worlds apart from the case of a genuinely tough question, where the teacher does believe that the presupposition is true but doesn't know whether he has the correct answer, or whether anyone else has. It is also different from the genuinely difficult recitation question to which the teacher knows the answer but the student isn't sure of knowing.) It is foregone that any answer to a trick question is wrong. After the student gives the necessarily wrong answer the teacher points out the correct answer, which invariably answers another question than the one asked, going on to point out the falsity of the presupposition that all had presumed to be true and believed that the teacher believed to be true, and which all students had to believe was true because willy-nilly they had to answer the question, willy-nilly with a wrong answer.

2. Answer

The distinctive feature of answers to recitation questions is not that they are correct/incorrect. For any answer to any question whatsoever might be a right answer or a wrong answer. Rather, it is that the correctness of answer has been predetermined before the asking and that, in general, there is but one answer that is predeterminately correct. Now, it may be that to any conceivable question there is one answer that is correct. But the presumption runs only that there be at least one correct answer; in many cases no one knows which of the alternative answers is the correct one; and in no case does someone know that. Thus in some cases people hold divergent answers; in some of these cases one of the answers is correct; and in certain of these cases it is known how to go about determining which of these answers is the correct one. None of this hemming and hawing stalls questions in recitation. There is but one answer that is correct; all respondents are to have that one correct answer; and that answer which is correct is already known, its correctness already determined. Elsewhere and otherwise that may be a wrong or a disputed or an alternative or an acceptable answer. But not in classroom recitation. For in recitation, there is immediate validation in the teacher's knowledge of that answer which is correct. (And there is further recourse to authoritative sources such as the textbook and the subject-matter specialists or other societies represented by the agency of the teacher.)

In classroom recitation it does not matter whether the question is factual or interpretive, simple or complex, lofty or base in cognition. Recitation is not a matter of fact only. It is a matter of knowledge that is predeterminately correct — for these purposes in this circumstance. The world may diverge on the reasons that Washington's army won the war against the British, or that the British army won the war against the French. But there is only one correct answer to the teacher's question, 'Why did Washington win?' The proof lies in what follows upon the answer.

3. Evaluation

The distinctive feature of the questioner's reaction to a recitation answer is that it evaluates the answer as either correct or incorrect, right or wrong. In other circumstances it may happen that the questioner does not react at all to the answer, or reacts other than with an evaluation, or reacts with an evaluation other than of the correctness of answer. For example, after the answer either the questioner or the respondent might go on to speak about something else; the questioner might acknowledge the answer ('Oh' or 'Thank you'); the questioner might evaluate the content of the answer, reacting to the information supplied ('Good news'). But none of that may happen in a classroom recitation, where it is obligatory that the teacher react with an evaluation of the rightness of the answer. Moreover, no one else in the room may do that, and the teacher may not choose to do something else. Nonetheless the teacher does have some elbow room in executing this forced manoeuvre. But if the teacher goes beyond these bonds, or yet fails to make the move in the first place, he will be quickly called to task and most immediately by the students themselves. They know what the teacher is supposed to do when a student has done what he is supposed to do by giving an answer to the question.

The basic way to perform this step is to say 'Right' or 'Wrong' and then, that done, to ask the next question. 'OK,' says Mr H, 'so France giving aid is an example of what?' If the teacher asks another question without saying 'Right,' it means the answer is right; if the teacher repeats the question or passes to another student without saying 'Wrong,' it means the answer is wrong. Everyone knows that, or at least they act as if they know that's the rule.

There are various ways of saying Right or Wrong. Right can be said as 'Right' or as 'Yes,' 'OK,' 'All right.' Wrong can be said as 'No', 'Not exactly,' 'Well,' 'But,' 'Not only that but,' and also as 'OK,' 'All right' plus repeat of question. Here are two examples.

   (a) What is nationalism?
      — X.
     All right, but what is it?
      — Y.
     Yeah, but what is it, basically? What is it?
      — It's a Z.
     All right, it's a Z. OK. It's a Z.
   (b) What do you see in this picture?
      — A.
     Yes, but what else do you see?
      — B.
     That's nice, and what do you see besides that?
      — I see a C.
     A C! Very good. C, it's a picture of C, does everyone see that?

These examples show that repeating the correct answer is a basic way of evaluating that it is right. In that way, perhaps, others in the room who might be paying attention can hear that this answer is the one correct answer for all. The correct answer may be repeated all by itself, firmly, or with these additions:

   (a) *confirmation.* 'DuQuesne, all right,' says Mr L. Others say: 'All right, X'; 'He was an X, right'; 'That's right, X'.

   (b) *emphasis.* To 'Mm-mm' in answer to 'Were they all interested?' Ms HT says, 'Sure, they were interested. They were all very much concerned.' Others say, 'All right, he certainly is an X'; 'All right, it's an X. OK, it's an X.' To 'Fur and fish' Mr L says, 'Fish and fur. Fish and furs.'

   (c) *elaboration.* When a student answers, 'The French were outnumbered,' Mr L says, 'The French were badly outnumbered, 20 to 1.' When he asks why overland travel took so long and someone answers 'Mountains,' he does not say 'No! You're wrong!' but 'Well, mountains. But what's the biggest thing, in a way?' When someone then answers 'Forest' he says 'Forest, it was solid forest.'

   (d) *praise.* Mr H says 'Aid from allies, very good.' Good teachers like Mr H are sparing with praise. Ordinary teachers lay it on, lauding every hapless pupil for each dumb answer which they then demonstrate to be wildly wrong by repeating the question or passing to another student who equally haplessly, perhaps, gives what turns out to be the right answer which in turn is heaped with praise equal to a wrong one. The extravagant praise commonly awarded to any pupil who will speak a syllable of recognizable response suggests that teachers want the pupils to speak, regardless; and that one broad purpose for their asking questions is just that, regardless of other purposes.

That may also explain why teachers seem loath to come right out and say 'No' or 'You're wrong', substituting in their stead such contraries as 'All right but . . .' and 'Not exactly' and 'Well but . . .'. So tricky must the evaluative move be that it is most commonly executed by entirely ignoring what the student has said, and passing on to another student who will say it right. The manoeuvre confirms before everyone's eyes the norm that what the students know, and most of what they say, *doesn't even matter*. Some child who says 'Thirty-five million' can be praised for the venture or passed over or patronized with a 'Not exactly' until the right answer of '0.214' is produced by someone else, knowingly or not. In both cases the teacher is also passing over the purpose for asking the question to begin with.

Since recitation is in essence a question-answer exchange, everything educational about it turns on how the teacher makes use of questions and what use he goes on to make of the answers.

USE OF QUESTIONS AND ANSWERS

The principle is *to use questions in service of pedagogical purpose in classroom circumstance*. Among the hundred or so techniques of questioning available for use in recitation, no more than one or two can serve all purposes in all circumstances. Rather than specify a multiplicity of techniques for multiple purposes and circumstances, identifying as well the sundry exceptions to each and every case in point, we may choose to entertain three pieces of practical advice for before, during, and after asking questions. That mercifully gives us only one thing to keep in mind at each step. But each one will require of us to discipline our behavior in an effort to serve our purposes in this circumstance.

In good service to purpose, the teacher chooses to prepare the questions beforehand, to ask them nice and slow, and to listen to the answers (see Figure 4.1). Only the more skilled questioners actually find it necessary or even useful to do any of that. They also find it tiresome. Beginners too may find it tiresome.

Prepare the questions

Before asking questions, prepare the questions to ask. Preparation involves us in the lofty pondering of the purposes we have in the circumstances we face, and conceiving of questions appropriate to circumstance and purpose. It also involves the sorry labor of writing the questions out until they strike us as right, and of arranging them in some promising order according to the series of answers we desire and anticipate. Preparation lastly includes the unfortunate task of testing the questions out (e.g., with a friend or spouse) to see whether other people make the same sense of the question as we intend, and whether they go on to give the kind of answers we anticipate. Only then will the questions be ready for the asking.

To help ourselves through this lonely period we might ask: 'What is it that students are to know or to learn from this lesson?' (e.g., from reading a chapter, completing an assignment, participating in a previous class or activity, or yet from the recitation itself). Then we take that answer and ask: 'To what questions does that knowledge or learning represent an answer?' That gives us the questions to prepare. They will be only a few in all, but we will have to write many versions before we get them right; and we might also write out the series of subordinate or related questions that lead up to or down from them.

That is not to say that we ought not to ask questions that appear to us at the moment good to ask, pursuing our purpose through the spontaneously developing traces of recitation. Rather it warns us that the traces can be lost, along with the purpose and point of the questions; and it leads us to appreciate how the suitable question prepared in advance may be introduced at the suitable juncture that develops, whereupon that question and not some others may be pursued through a series of subordinate questions.

As it is, people commonly just ask and answer numbers of questions that come to mind, bringing them wherever the questions happen to lead and then leaving them at that odd point. Then the teacher often leaves off the asking and launches, as Mr H does (Appendix), a short lecture trying to make the point that the question-answers clearly did not. Better to prepare the questions beforehand.

Figure 4.1: Pedagogy of recitation questions

Based on Teacher Questions	Based on Student Questions
Prepare the questions to ask	*Preparation*
1. Write them down until right 2. Arrange them in a promising order 3. Try them on friends, then revise	Have *students prepare five written questions and answers,* while you prepare ten questions
Ask questions nice and slow	*Exchange*
1. Stop and think 2. Ask and stop	Help *students orally exchange their questions and answers,* while you listen and comment
Listen to the answers	1. Student A asks a question 2. Student B gives an answer 3. Student A evaluates the answer 4. Student B asks the next question
1. Listen for the forthcoming answer 2. Listen for all the answer that is forthcoming 3. Listen to right and wrong answers, from dumb and smart students	*Quiz*
	Contribute a few of your questions, to be answered or not orally or in writing
	Evaluation
	Evaluate the question-answers, correcting the questions and teaching students to use questions for learning

Ask questions nice and slow

When asking questions, go nice and slow. 'Nice' refers to tone and attitude, 'slow' to frequency and pace. Little educative purpose is served by asking questions furiously, even in a recitation designed merely to test students' knowledge.

If the teacher's purpose is to find out what students know, then one nice attitude to express via the manner of asking is 'interestedness', asking as if you were interested in what they know. And a slow pace lets you find that out, by giving them time to say what they know and by giving you time to handle what they say — appreciating it, reacting to it, making sure of it. Often enough people do not know what they are saying in answer although they know perfectly well how to answer the question. The teacher whose purpose it is to find out the student's knowledge does well to slow down long enough to find that out. Until then no purpose is served by asking another question.

To help ourselves slow down so that we can achieve our purpose for asking, we can stop and think before asking and then ask and stop.

Stop and think reminds us not to ask the question that pops into our mind but to give it at least a passing moment's reflection and formulation. Then it has more of a chance of being an educative question rather than an everyday one. Everyday questions are easy to come by and easy to ask. The educative questions are harder. They must be disciplined to purpose through reflection and for-mulation, even if only on second thought before the moment of asking.

Ask and stop reminds us not to go on asking another question once we ask the question that we have just stopped and thought about the moment before (or prepared long beforehand). That helps us to avoid comically-frustrating habits such as asking run-on questions:

> What did the colonists think about England? They probably felt what? What did England do for the colonists? Tina. A lot or very little? How do you think the colonists felt? Do you think they did a lot for them?

In answer to this interrogative panoply, Tina elects to say 'No.' Mr L confirms this answer to his last question while proceeding to answer his first or second one. 'No, they felt . . .' By asking and then stopping we also save ourselves from (1) repeating our question, (2) repeating the question and then asking its opposite, and (3) answering our own question.

1. Why did the English eventually win the war? Why did the English eventually win the war?
2. And how would you do that? And how would you fight the Indians? Or, how did the Indians fight?
3. They just wanted to be here, period. Why? Didn't like it over there. What reason? Tom. Why didn't they like it over there?

These examples from a teacher with 26 years of experience help us to appreciate the difficulty of asking questions rightly, as well as the very simplicity of it. Anyone can see that no purpose is served, and some purpose frustrated, by answering your own questions, repeating them, and running on with them.

There is no trick to these matters. Any teacher can sit down and list out a dozen techniques of questioning; and you as well as other teachers can stand up in your classroom and figure out which techniques to use for serving your purposes in your circumstances. And too, you as well as the experienced teachers in these examples may well do it wrongly in the heat of the exchange. But you will be doing quite well by asking nicely and slowly the questions you have laboriously prepared beforehand, and then by listening carefully to the answers.

Listen to the answers

After asking the question, listen to the answer. That is the one essential thing to do with answers. It is a simple behaviour that seems to require uncommon discipline. And it takes time.

Without disciplining your behaviour during this time, you may instead of listening to the answer find yourself busy with other pressing matters such as thinking up the next question to ask. As one immediate result you may go on to ask the wrong question or teach the wrong lesson; for, you may have missed the answer or overlooked what it reveals of the student's mind. To find that out may have been your purpose for asking. By now taking the time and care to listen, you can discover how the answer is serving that purpose. You can see what kind of answer is forthcoming, and you can come to appreciate the student's state of mind or knowledge that led to the answer. Also you can look to see whether what has followed upon the question is an answer at all or just one of the numerous acceptable ways of responding to a question without answering it.

These and other things to do with the answer will take time. In the meantime it serves no purpose to ask the next question. That would move the recitation right along but leave purposes behind, likely with most of the pupils. Better to stay with the pupils, lingering for a moment to listen to the answer.

It may surprise us to learn that both wrong and right answers and smart and dumb pupils bear listening to. Teachers do tend to accept right answers and to reject wrong ones, in either case moving rapidly onto the next question or to the next student. You, however, might prefer to stay a bit with both kinds of answer given by both types of pupil, until such time as you have *appreciated the knowledge* that led either pupil to give either answer.

Answers on the face of them do not reveal knowledge. For instance, the child who gives a wrong answer may rightly be answering in his mind a somewhat different question, or may otherwise reasonably be answering wrongly; while a correct answer can easily be supplied by a pupil who knows well the words and ways of answering questions but who nonetheless knows imperfectly if at all the stuff and substance of the thing in answer. If among your purposes for asking questions you design to discover what students know so as to teach them rightly to know, you will sensibly stay a while with the pupil and listen to the answer. It is only a matter of seconds, one or two at that.

Staying and listening also helps us wait a bit for the answer that may be forthcoming. It is a strange fact of classroom life that pupils are habitually given far less than a second to come up with an answer, and are habituated to encapsulating their answers in staccato bursts punctuated by teacher questions. If you prefer, you may listen for the answer that is forthcoming and for all of it that will come. In that way you may hear an answer that otherwise would remain unheard for failure to appear within the millisecond. You may hear more of an answer than otherwise allotted by truncation. And you may hear a further or other answer than otherwise allowed, as the pupil qualifies, corrects, re-starts and reformulates the bits and pieces ejaculated at the panicky start, including the usual bit of 'I don't know.' To hear these is most necessary to purpose, where purpose is to find out what students know.

On the other hand, if purpose is to get the questions answered or the material covered, then there is no use to staying and listening.

Rather move along with the questions. Two or three people in the room can always be counted on to do the right thing and supply the answers so that the questions can continue on their untrammeled way. In that way many question-answers will be performed and much ground covered, and the recitation will in the end have achieved its purpose irrespective of the pupils and their knowledge.

Far better to stay a while and tend to the answers. This is a disciplined and timely behavior before going on to act rightly on the answers by asking the next apt question of the moment or by designing the apt lesson of the morrow. In good service to purpose in circumstance, the teacher does well to prepare the questions beforehand, to ask them nice and slow, and to listen to the answers.

AN ALTERNATIVE RECITATION

An alternative approach is to conduct a recitation by means of questions from *students*. The details of this approach will vary as suitable to circumstance, around an essential process of student questioning and answering wherein students recite what they know and are coming to know.

In outline, the approach moves through four basic phases (see Figure 4.2).

1. *Preparation*. Students as well as teacher prepare questions.
2. *Exchange*. Students exchange their questions and answers.
3. *Quiz*. The teacher contributes questions.
4. *Evaluation*. The teacher evaluates the question-answers.

The approach has many variations, combinations, options, and the like. One way of enacting this approach will be described as an example, not an exemplar. The few basic things that must be done will be specified, the basic principles identified, and some of the possible details filled in.

Preparation

As before, the first thing to do is to prepare the questions for asking. Here students as well as teacher prepare questions, for students too will be asking them.

The questions bear as usual on the subject-matter at hand — a previous lesson or activity, an assignment completed, a movie, field-trip or other experience, a textbook read. As appropriate to circumstance, students may spend the night at home crafting a list for the morrow, or they may spend a few moments in class sketching the questions to be asked next. For example, the students have read a chapter or a story in their book and they prepare questions to ask during the class recitation next day. That night the teacher too prepares questions as usual but fewer of them, perhaps ten in all.

From the reading each student formulates five questions and answers, writing them down on a 'recitation paper' or other list. These five will turn out to be points that caught the student's attention, struck his interest, seemed somehow important or useful to know. (It later proves most helpful to have noted the page number as well. Surprisingly many questions cannot be answered by anyone else in the room.) The students are not playing teacher but student, asking the question that comes naturally to their mind and study. For one of the questions, 5, the student permissibly writes no answer because it is a matter that he is not sure of and he would like to hear other people's answer. It is not a question for discussion but for recitation, answerable like all the others from the reading.

The principle quietly at work here is that these five question-answers represent five things that the student actually knows (whether correctly or not, wisely or not), on the view that our knowledge consists in our question-answer propositions. A teacher might be tickled pink that students know five things from every lesson. Other teachers will hold out for knowing the 50 statements in the book. But no one can know any statement without knowing the question to which the statement is an answer. Perhaps then the teacher will assign 50 question-answers to be written. The more experienced teacher modestly takes pleasure in the thought that the student knows against all odds five things for a start, while anticipating more to come in the recitation. Still, the teacher will have to discover which five point are known, by whom, and how well. The students' questions supply the device for finding that out. Whence the teacher's choice to conduct the recitation by means of student questions.

As time goes along the teacher will help students to formulate and to use questions. But at this point only one instruction is given, to ask simple questions answerable from the reading and above all not to ask fancy questions. Smart questions are ruled out. The teacher hopes that the class matures to the point where students will roll their eyes and mutter 'Oh, no, what a smart question!' Gradually the normative reaction becomes 'Thank goodness, a dumb question — I know that one!' As a rule of thumb, the teacher advises students to write questions that anyone who has given a good try at the reading can have a decent chance of answering. Everyone soon discovers that the dullest and plainest of questions lead to interesting interactions and decorative learning.

Exchange

In class, students orally exchange their questions and answers. For several delicate reasons the exchange must begin with a student question and it must not begin with a teacher question. The basic exchange runs:

1. Student A asks a question.
2. Student B gives an answer.
3. Student A evaluates the answer.
4. Student B asks the next question.

In this single process two students are each doing two different things in complement: A asks and replies, B answers and asks. In the usual approach to recitation, only one student is doing something and only the one thing, answering. What is more, in the alternative approach the basic exchange quickly gets even further involved.

The process takes on its own form and momentum as students manage the exchange and engage in various ways by contributing related questions, answers, and evaluations. For example, student C will say that she had the same question as A but a different answer; or D tells of a similar answer to B but a different question. Thus at step 2 there may be answers from C as well as from B, which A must evaluate in stepping back and forth at step 3. When all are satisfied, the student who has given the last or best answer goes on to ask the next question, usually prefacing it with 'Here's a question related to that,' or some such phrase.

There is no fuss or bother to any of this. It is a normal and smooth if complicated process that every ordinary speaker of the language is competent to engage in, and indeed does engage in — except in classrooms. Only in the first few turns or days will the teacher have to remind the students to do what otherwise comes naturally, staying alert and actually speaking back and forth with the person who you are talking with.

Experienced pupils — those with two or more years of schooling — will hesitate to start, and to start with a question. Some student must volunteer to start, otherwise the process will never begin (a teacher question will not start this process but another).

Having contributed the question, the questioner and everyone else will look down at their papers and books, awaiting the teacher's notification of who is to give the answer. They must look up at each other, questioner and respondents, so that respondents can identify themselves and the questioner can choose among them.

At the next step, while giving their answer, experienced students will turn and face the teacher, who must gently turn them to speak to the person whose question they are answering while also turning the questioner to other students who are signalling to the teacher that they too wish to speak to the questioner.

The answer to his question having been given, the retiring questioner next needs a gentle reminder to come forth with a reply to the respondent and, in replying, actually to evaluate the answer according to his sense. Lastly the winning respondent will appreciate a gentle nudge to ask the next question.

All of this will need doing but only in the first few rounds. The behavior is normal and to be expected of people accustomed to teacher questioning, while the new behavior is also perfectly normal and to be expected of people accustomed to everyday language. The turn-taking mechanism will take care of itself, once students realize which mechanism is being invoked here. Young pupils can manage this recitation process, just as they can the other; and older students too can manage, although with greater difficulty and embarrassment at the start.

At all times the teacher remains in control, as all in the room know full well. For the moment he is lending support and help in the process. But the teacher's primary role is to *listen*. And that is quite enough to do as an active, disciplined pedagogical behavior in service of purpose in this circumstance.

To listen is the teacher's primary role because the first purpose is to discover and to appreciate the students' knowledge of the subject-matter in question. There are a lot of students out there and many exchanges going on; knowledge wafts and fleets. Amidst it all the teacher attends and listens. By catching the question-answer proposition that students are forming of the subject-matter he discovers what they know, and by following the question-answer relations in those propositions he discovers what they understand and mean.

The teacher's secondary role is to intervene, basing appropriate action on the appreciation thus formed of students' present knowledge, understanding, and meaning. As the process continues the teacher, as ever the case, has the right to talk at any step; and he chooses aptly to step in with instructive comments, rarely with a question. For example, the teacher points out relations among the exchanges, missing connections between question and answer, other possible evaluative replies, alternative answers and alternative formulations of the question; he elaborates on selected points not well understood, makes applications to past and future lessons, and reconstructs series and summaries of question-answer propositions thus far.

After the teacher has finished his instructive intervention the students, as ever is the case in this recitation, have the next turn at talk. Thanks to the turn-taking mechanism everyone now knows who the next speaker is to be, what the speaker is supposed to do next, and who the speaker is to do that with. Depending on where they are in the ongoing exchange, the last respondent asks the next question, or the questioner evaluates the answer, or the respondent gives an answer, or the questioner reformulates and reposes the question, often adding 'Well, the reason I asked this is because on the other page . . .' or some such phrase that nicely leads to a still more involving exchange.

Thus the exchange is not always a straightforward 1–2–3 affair but often involves repeated back-and-forth steps of 1, of 2, of 3. It commonly happens that question and answer are negotiated and reformulated as they are exchanged.

For example, student A asks a perfectly clear and simple question that, upon the answering, turns out to be muddled and complex. In cooperative interaction with students B and C, student A reformulates the question until it makes the sense as originally intended and/or as now shared by B and C. Now there are actually at least two questions, each question to be fitted with a suitable answer. Whereas before there was the original Q1 with a subsequent A2, now A1 is found for Q1 and Q2 for A2.

Equally often it happens that the answer is muddled and complex, whereupon the two questions that it addresses are identified and the pieces of answer sorted out. The same may happen with the evaluation given in the third step.

All of that goes to show that the exchange is not a matter of two students asking and answering one question. More than two students get involved in the one question; more than one question gets involved; and more than question and answer get involved. The principle is that students are exhibiting their knowledge of the subject-matter, forming and then re-forming it in a mutual exchange of meanings and understandings as they negotiate their question-answer propositions. The pedagogy is to listen and then intervene to help students form suitable propositions of the subject-matter set for recitation.

As a result of this rich exchange and teaching, each student knows better the five points prepared on his recitation paper, and he knows further five or ten others that emerged in the process. The students know these things because it is by students that the question-answer propositions are formed, in a student-student exchange that involves the student more and involves more students, various students in each exchange and each student in various exchanges, all playing in turn different active roles as they resolve their knowledge of the subject-matter.

Quiz

Quiz is the phase wherein the teacher contributes questions. The phase begins at a point where the teacher judges that the students have formed a sufficient measure of grounded knowledge of the subject-matter. That is, enough questions have been asked and answered rightly by enough students. Or maybe the time is up. Now it is time for the teacher to ask questions.

The quiz may be oral or written. If written, it continues on the students' recitation paper, with the first teacher question as 6 on the paper. The questions are selected from the teacher's prepared list of ten questions, perhaps with one or two of particular note selected from the preceding exchange.

Ordinarily, many of the ten questions on the teacher's list will already have surfaced during the exchange. Some will figure on the list prepared by various students; one will be posed aloud by some student; another will be identified spontaneously in the course of dealing with a related question; for still another the teacher has blurted 'Oh, good, that was one of my questions too,' or some such phrase.

Perhaps five questions from the teacher are enough, 6–10 on the recitation paper. It may further be enough that the students write down only the questions, without having also to answer them. The teacher may wish to contribute questions alone as a way of alerting students to points they may have missed, things they should know or know better, or items that otherwise would have been covered had there been more time for the exchange. Then the students will have a good note of them on their papers and might find the answers later, or at least have a better chance of keeping them in mind. Experienced students will have a time of it not filling in the answers; questions beg for answers, and 1–5 on the paper are already nicely filled in according to form. The teacher's questions now dangle.

Evaluation

The remaining phase is to evaluate the question-answers. The evaluation may be oral or written; it may bear on written and/or oral questions on student papers, in the exchange, or during the quiz; it may be given on the spot or later, and individually or corporately. Evaluation must be fitted in somewhere as part of the recitation, and it is the teacher's enduring responsibility to supply it.

The teacher supplies evaluation during the exchange as he listens to appreciate the students' expressed knowledge and then intervenes to comment and to correct it. If an oral quiz follows the exchange, the teacher evaluates the oral answers as they are given. If the quiz is written, the teacher can rehearse the question-answers immediately thereafter or collect the papers for later written evaluation. Scores or grade points can be assigned or not for the quiz, as desired, perhaps giving the students five points for their five question-answers before going on to score 6–10 (where also answered).

Whether the quiz has been oral or written, and whether the questions have been answered or not and orally or not evaluated, the teacher may now collect the papers for later evaluation and instruction of each individual student. At this point the teacher corrects the *questions*. For example, he comments on phrasing and structure; identifies underlying assumptions and divergent meanings; suggests alternative formulations; and traces the interrelations among various pieces of question and answer.

All of this is to instruct the student on how to formulate and use questions for studying and learning. This is precious teaching, and with it the recitation is complete.

This alternative approach to recitation serves some purposes and not others. So too the usual approach. How nice it would be if beginning teachers got a good start, doing things aptly to begin with, by making of this alternative approach the usual while using the usual approach as an occasional alternative.

By contrast to the usual approach, this alternative recitation takes greater effort and more time, while covering less ground or subject-matter. On the other hand it makes time for students to think and to speak, it frees the teacher to listen and to instruct, and it secures the ground that it does cover.

Moreover, the alternative approach supplies a mechanism for systematic and extensive student participation, ensuring not only that students speak in turn but also that various students speak in each exchange and each student speaks in various roles. It further carries learners through an active and cooperative dynamics from the very start and even before, as students too prepare and ask questions, initiate and direct exchanges, negotiate and evaluate answers, form and re-form their knowledge.

Above all the approach locates and exhibits for the teacher's appreciation and intervention the precise state of mind of the students, what they know of the subject-matter and how they know it. This it does at every step on all points for each student through the student question-answer proposition that is knowledge. Thus teachers who aspire to use some approximation of a genuinely Socratic method might well enact Socrates' proposal that we educate our young to become masters of asking and answering questions (*Republic* VII.534). Enacting this alternative recitation is one good turn towards that mastery and the learning that results.

CORRELATED READINGS

A Education

Collins, A. (1977) 'Processes in acquiring knowledge', in R.C. Anderson, R.J. Spiro, and W.E. Montague (eds.), *Schooling and the acquisition of knowledge*, Hillsdale, N.J.: Erlbaum, 339–363; Collins, A. and Stevens, A.L. (1982) 'Goals and strategies of inquiry teachers', in R. Glaser (ed.), *Advances in instructional psychology II*, Hillsdale, N.J.: Erlbaum, 65–119 — a *tour de force*, the only one of its kind, defining precisely what the 'Socratic method' is as teachers use it, in terms of specific rules and strategies of questioning at each and every point, illustrated with actual classroom examples.

Dillon, J.T. (1978) 'Using questions to depress student thought', *School Review*, 87, 50–64; Dillon, J.T. (1982) 'The effect of questions in education and other enterprises', *Journal of Curriculum Studies*, 14, 127–152 — an argumentative essay and a review giving theoretical, empirical, and practical reasons that teacher questions do not stimulate students' cognitive, affective, and expressive processes.

Dillon, J.T. (1980) 'Curiosity as non-sequitur of Socratic questioning', *Journal of Educational Thought*, *14*, 17–22; Dillon, J.T. (1980) '*Paper Chase* and the Socratic method of teaching law', *Journal of Legal Education*, *30*, 529–535 — analysis of how Socrates used questions and the effect on his interlocutors, by contrast to the questions and effects of teachers' so-called Socratic method.

Fitch, J.G. (1879) *The art of questioning*, Chicago: Flanagan — a short, old manual, originally talks to teachers, as good as any manual published over the past 100 years — save of course for this present one.

Gall, M.D. (1984) 'Synthesis of research on teachers' questioning', *Educational Leadership*, *42*(3), 40–47 — an easy review, for teachers, of studies conducted since 1970 on recitation questions.

Hoetker, J. and Ahlbrand, W. (1969) 'The persistence of the recitation', *American Educational Research Journal*, *6*, 145–167 — a review of studies to 1950 on recitation questions, together with a study of recitation in secondary classrooms.

Johnson, M.C. (1979) *Discussion dynamics*, Rowley, MA: Newbury — an unnoticed little book that is the best sociolinguistic study of recitation dynamics, the detailed moves and meanings of question-answer in actual elementary and secondary classrooms.

Stevens, R. (1912) 'The question as a measure of efficiency in instruction: A critical study of class-room practice', *Teachers College Contributions to Education*, No. 48, New York: Teachers College Press — an oldie but goodie, one of the first and most fascinating studies of recitation, in actual secondary classrooms.

Stodolsky, S.S., Ferguson, T.L., and Wimpelberg, K. (1981) 'The recitation persists, but what does it look like?', *Journal of Curriculum Studies*, *13*, 121–130 — a detailed observational study of the purposes, behaviors, and materials of recitation in elementary math and social studies classrooms at different socioeconomic levels.

B Other fields

Buckwalter, A. (1983) *Interviews and interrogations*, Stoneham, MA: Butterworth — a fascinating manual for private investigators, with completely surprising techniques for questioning criminal suspects and others in order to find out all the truthful information they know.

Dillon, J.T. (1986) 'Questioning', in O. Hargie (ed.), *A handbook of communication skills*, London: Croom Helm, 95–127 — a comprehensive review on using the elements of questioning and answering as a communicative skill in various practical contexts.

Kestler, J. (1982) *Questioning techniques and tactics*, Colorado Springs, CO: Shepard's/McGraw-Hill — hundreds of practical techniques for courtroom lawyers for putting questions to people who are forced to answer but don't want to tell the truth of what they know.

Payne, S.L. (1951) *The art of asking questions*, Princeton, N.J.: Princeton University; Sudman, S. and Bradburn, N. (1982) *Asking questions: A practical guide to questionnaire design*, San Francisco: Jossey-Bass — detailed practical advice, in an easy style with humorous examples, from classic and contemporary authorities on how to formulate and to ask questions in order to get reliable answers from respondents in surveys and opinion polls.

Santas, G.X. (1979) *Socrates*. London: Routledge & Kegan Paul, 59–96 — a masterly analysis of the master of questioning.

Schuman, H. and Presser, S. (1981) *Questions and answers in attitude surveys*, New York: Academic — 200 experiments on the effects of various forms, wordings, and sequences of questions in national surveys, showing the different answers that people give to different forms of the same questions, etc.

Woodbury, H. (1984) 'The strategic use of questions in court', *Semiotica*, *48*, 197–228 — an absorbing study of questions put during a murder trial, showing how each attorney uses the same types of questions in systematically different ways with different witnesses during different parts of the trial process.

PRACTICAL EXERCISES

1. Conduct a recitation on this chapter

With the concurrence of your instructor and five or so congenial classmates, conduct a 15-minute recitation on this chapter. You and a fellow student might each conduct a recitation, each with a different group of students. Thereafter the whole class can discuss your recitation, or compare and discuss the two recitations, exploring the purposes, circumstances, questions and knowledge in each case.

Perhaps you and a classmate can use either the traditional approach to recitation or the alternative recitation, in either case following the recommendations of this chapter. Thereafter the whole class can discuss the two different approaches or the two different versions of each approach.

2. Practise identifying questions

Identify and formulate in writing the overall question that this chapter answers, together with the questions answered by each of the various parts or sections. Compare your questions point for point with those identified by classmates.

3. Practise preparing questions

Make a list of ten written questions, arranged in some promising order, that you judge useful to ask in a recitation over the subject-matter of this chapter. Compare your questions, their ordering and their particular formulation with those of your classmates, or with those actually asked in Exercise 1.

4. Practise testing questions

Dream up any question you like about anything you want. Write it out. Put the question to any three people who you think actually have an answer to it. Take note of the problems that each respondent has in understanding the question that you put and intend, and in giving comparable answers to it. Rewrite the question accordingly. Repeat Exercise 4.

5. Relate purposes and questions

As a variant of these exercises, merely identify the purpose that you judge should be served in a recitation over this chapter, and then identify those questions and questioning techniques that would (a) serve this purpose and (b) serve not this but other purposes.

As still a further variant, list out (a) the purposes that might be served and (b) those that cannot be served, by the alternative approach recommended in this chapter. Go on to elaborate all the disadvantages and advantages of any kind that you can attribute to the alternative approach. Discuss your list with classmates, or compare your list to theirs.

Get other students to join in the exercise by doing the same on the traditional or usual approach to recitation, then compare various lists for the two approaches.

6. Identify questioning techniques

Make a list of ten detailed questioning techniques suitable to recitation. Arrange them in order of importance or usefulness. Add ten more that are not at all suitable in your judgment. Compare your 'do's' and 'don'ts' to those of fellow students, and together construct a better list.

Then examine the list together, crossing off all techniques that do not apply in this or that circumstance of recitation. Or add to each item all the 'if's', 'and's' and 'but's' that are needed.

Defend your list against this challenging proposition: *No specific question or questioning technique can be used in all recitations, given various purposes and circumstances.*

7. Evaluate advice on questioning

Read any manual on teacher questioning, any chapter on questioning in a teacher-education or methods text, or any article on questioning in the pedagogical literature (that is, not research reports or theoretical models but advice to teachers). State good grounds for dismissing each piece of advice, each technique recommended. Or list out all the exceptions that you must take to each point by imagining diverse purposes and circumstances in classroom recitations.

Do this exercise on the advice given in this present chapter. Discuss your evaluation with classmates, or compare your several evaluations of the same piece of advice or the same manual, etc.

8. Analyze recitations

Three different recitations are illustrated in the Appendix (Mr H, Mrs HT, Mr L), and several snippets from other recitations are illustrated in the text of this chapter. Take any point, large or small, from this chapter or from any of the readings or yet from any of these exercises, and work the point through the illustrated recitations. Report your analysis and let your classmates discuss it, and compare yours to theirs.

9. Do it to friends and betters

In any social circumstance, start talking to your friends in questions. Count how many questions you manage to ask before they stop you. Ask a question of a social superior and see if you can get away with asking one or two more. In both cases note the colorful ways they stop you.

114

Turn next to a child and see if anything at all save your fatigue can stop your questions. Note the minimal answers.

10. Imitate Socrates

Especially with a friend, and only from a pedagogical and not philosophical perspective, read these selected Dialogues by Plato — the *Apology*, *Charmides*, *Lysis*, *Laches*. Discover the questions that Socrates used, his manner of asking them, the people and circumstances of asking, the motive and purpose, the effect and result.

Marshalling your discoveries, attempt to refute this unassailable proposition: *Socrates' method is beyond the personal character and professional capacity of you and most other teachers to learn and to use.* Perhaps you and your friend or fellow student could examine this proposition together in a Socratic dialogue before the class or over a few drinks. If drinking, read the *Symposium* too.

5

Questioning and Discussion

OVERVIEW

CHARACTERISTICS OF DISCUSSION
A characteristic discussion: Mr T's history lesson
Characteristic talk
Characteristic questions

USE OF QUESTIONS
Discussion question
Perplexity questions

USE OF ALTERNATIVES
Statements
    Declarative statement
    Reflective restatement
    Statement of mind
    Statement of interest
    Student referral
    Teacher reddition
Student questions
    Speaker's question
    Class question
    Discussion question
Signals
    Phatics
    Fillers
    Pass

116

Silences
    Deliberate silence
    Non-deliberate silence

USING QUESTIONS AND ALTERNATIVES

Service to purpose
    Learning to discuss
    Fostering discussion
    Learning subject-matter
Choice of action
Reflection on enacted choice

CORRELATED READINGS

PRACTICAL EXERCISES

Figure 5.1: Pedagogy of discussion questions
Figure 5.2: Alternatives to questioning

Questioning and Discussion

As with recitation, the use of questions during discussion is disciplined to serve pedagogical purpose in classroom circumstances. Purpose and circumstance here call for a special style of questioning behavior on the part of both teacher and students, a style entirely different from questioning in recitation. Everyone will have to learn and practice this distinct style of questioning if they are to join in a discussion.

Although discussion resembles recitation in that students and teachers are talking back and forth, discussion is a process with characteristics of its own, entailing a characteristic use of questions to facilitate the process. Therefore, the use of questions appropriate to recitation promises only to foil discussion, turning it into something like a recitation. In service of discussion, the teacher disciplines his questioning behavior in two complementary ways.

First, the teacher uses only two broad types of questions, and relatively few questions in all. He poses the question for discussion; and he asks questions that perplex self.

Second, in place of other non-discussion questioning behaviors, the teacher chooses to use a range of non-questioning alternatives. He makes various kinds of statements; provides for student questions; gives attentive signals; and maintains deliberate silences. Using a mix of these alternatives together with the occasional self-perplexing question and the single well-chosen question for discussion promises to serve educational purpose in this circumstance by enhancing the students' cognitive, affective, and expressive processes while modeling appropriate discussion behaviors for students to imitate. The result is good discussion.

Although the questioning differs in this case, the pedagogy of questioning remains the same. The teacher uses questions and alternatives in service to purpose and circumstance, making choices for action and reflecting on enacted choice. The answer to 'What is the effective use of questions during discussion?' will be found in practice.

To inform practice we shall here first describe the *characteristics of discussion*, next recommend two *uses of questions* and then a dozen *uses of alternatives*, lastly reviewing the pedagogy of *using questions and alternatives* during discussion.

119

CHARACTERISTICS OF DISCUSSION

'Discussion' is a rubric embracing an ill-defined range of classroom activities wherein students and teacher talk back and forth over some matter at issue. When the process exhibits certain features we ascribe to it the character of discussion. Among the most noticeable characteristics are those describing the talk that is exchanged and the questions that are asked. To illustrate, here is a characteristic discussion, an example of one of several kinds of discussion. (Examples of other kinds are given in the Appendix.)

A characteristic discussion

In this episode, Mr T's history class turns to discuss Louis XIV's treatment of Huguenot dissenters.

T: The treatment that Louis XIV gave to the Huguenots is anything but acceptable, and yet some people say that he was justified in his treatment of the Huguenots, in respect to the point that he was trying to take care of his country. Do you feel that Louis was justified in his treatment of the Huguenots? — Rosa.

Rosa: I think, you know, they had their religion and stuff like that. I don't think he should have gone as far as totally kicking them out of the country and giving them, like, social disgrace, you know, like taking their jobs away from them. If they wouldn't interfere with his way of ruling, and their religion, why should he interfere with them? [T: Ken.]

Ken: He's partially right in what he did, but I don't feel he should've kicked them out, like she said. 'Cause who is he to say how they can — you know? Even though it's all Catholics, he gave 'em, like, religious freedom. [T: Barb.]

Barb: I feel, I feel that he had hardly any justification at all. He wound up at the end, as Lydia said, having to almost be persuaded by all the people around him that were saying, 'Well, look at the Huguenots.' You know, 'Why don't you do something about the Huguenots? We don't like the Huguenots.' [continues] It was one of the last places that he had to conquer, so he figured he'd just go out and then kill 'em. I think it was totally unfair.

T: OK, I can see where you're coming from, but I don't know

if I can totally agree with that. Is there anyone who disagrees with what these people are saying? — Marty.

Marty: I don't really disagree, but you know, we know the story, how everything worked out. [continues] They wanted to get rid of the Huguenots. And just like that, you know, us here, we don't like somebody, like, you know, Italians and Nazis — sorta the same thing, something like that, in their eyes. I don't think he was justified himself. [T: Diane.]

Diane: OK, in those days the church and state were like the same thing and everything, and so I think, well, like Louis — well, it isn't like today, when you can be a member of a country, just a member of a country. In those days, the church and the country meant the same thing, and when he saw people breaking away from the church, then he thought that they were breaking away from him. And he wanted to stop it. That was about the only thing he could do.

T: So you feel that he was justified in what he was doing, as far as he was concerned — he could justify it to himself.

Diane: Yeah, he could justify it to himself. But then, before then they really didn't have a separation. So all he could see was an allegory. And he wanted to pull back on that.

T: All right, Marty raised an interesting point just a few seconds ago. He said that [continues about Communists and Nazis in Chicago]. It's getting away from France, but again it's speaking about the same idea — acceptance of groups that are going against the norms of your society. What's your opinion on groups of this type? Should they be allowed, should they be censored, should it be washed over, should there be guidelines, stipulations — should there be control like Louis XIV tried to control them, to be done away with? — Julie.

Julie: I think that they should be allowed to speak their opinion, because [continues]. But they should be allowed to speak their opinion, you don't have to listen. [T: OK, Sean.]

Sean: I think Marty was wrong, because [continues]. Look what they did like, back I think in the 50s with the Communists, and McCarthy, and then during World War II with the Japanese. So, it's still going on today.

T: Right, and the concentration camps which we have had inside the United States during World War II, to house Japanese-Americans because you couldn't trust the Japanese. All right, so he's totally disagreeing with what you had to say, Marty.

Marty: Yeah, well — No, he brought up a good point. [continues] But I mean, I don't think Thomas Jefferson and those guys who signed the Constitution would like Nazis around here. Especially after what they did. I think that's why —

Steve: They come over here from another country for three months and they earn a ADC [welfare] check! My parents have been working for 25 some odd years, and they're not getting half the money that [ethnic epithet] are getting nowadays.

T: Yes, we know [continues].

One of the most noticeable features of this talk is that the teacher does not speak at every turn but yields the floor to a second and a third student speaker. Most striking of all, the teacher does not speak in questions at every turn. He poses one at the start to define the issue for discussion, and another at midpoint to redirect it. In their turn, students speak at considerable length, referring to one another's contributions and introducing 'outside' topics and materials as they form their understanding of the issue in past and present terms. Most of these features will be seen in any discussion. None will be seen in a recitation.

For example, let us contrast Mr T's discussion with the recitation in Mr H's history class (illustrated in the previous chapter, p. 88). Mr H speaks at every turn, and usually speaks in questions. Students therefore speak in answers, speaking only to the teacher and never to or about another student or idea. Both episodes have the same number of exchanges. The selection for Mr T's discussion lasts seven minutes, by contrast to less than one minute for the whole of Mr H's recitation episode. The entire recitation has already transpired in the time that it takes for a single exchange in the discussion. There are not five questions during the whole discussion, compared with questions every five seconds in the recitation. Finally, when students speak, their answers in the recitation last one second compared with one minute for their contributions in the discussion. Thus in each case there is a characteristic kind of talk, marked especially by a characteristic use of questions.

Characteristic talk

Those characteristics which are of the essence of discussion are easily enough stated but next to impossible to observe with your own eyes and ears. They have to do with the dispositions and attitudes of participants, together with the logical and epistemological conditions of the process in which they are disposed to engage. Happily for us, however, discussion also exhibits distinctive features of *talk* that follow in some way from the essential characteristics and make plain to us that we are in a discussion rather than a recitation. (We will bear in mind that there are essential characteristics other than talk and characteristics of talk other than noticeable ones.)

The first and most striking feature is seen in the *exchange of talk*. The characteristic exchange in recitation is question and answer from teacher and student. That is *not* characteristic of discussion. Discussion features a mix of statements and questions from a mix of students and teacher. The pace of the exchange is slower in discussion and it cannot be fast; there are fewer and longer exchanges, especially when students speak. In recitation there are many brief exchanges, especially when students answer; the pace can permissibly be leisurely but it is typically fast. Overall, the teacher contributes at least two-thirds of the talk exchanged in recitation, whereas in discussion students contribute half or more of the talk. That follows from the turn-taking involved in the characteristic exchange.

The *turn at talk* is noticeably different. At each turn in a recitation, the speaker and the move are predictable, as if the cycle were obligatory: teacher question, student answer, teacher evaluation plus next question. In discussion the cycles are optional and the speaker and move are not predictable. Although the teacher still retains the right to speak at any and every turn, the cycle may begin with a student instead of a teacher and it may continue with student or with teacher; while the speaker, teacher or student, may ask a question or not, give an answer or not, evaluate or not the previous speaker's move. Discussion features a mix of moves, a mix of speakers plus moves, and a mix of cycles with mixed speakers and moves.

To gain a concrete sense of this abstract mix, you might list out the possibilities: cycles of two, three, and four steps; speakers T or S at each step; and moves of Q or non-Q by each speaker at each step, along with A and non-A, and E and non-E. Recitation is always a case of the one cycle with three steps involving speakers T–S–T and moves Q–A–E in that invariant order. You may see just that in a discussion, but you will also see other cycles, speakers, moves; in a recitation you will see just that and only that.

There follows a third overall difference, in *sequence of student talk*. This difference is obvious enough from considering the previous feature but only now does it become more noticeable. In general, there will be no student-student sequences in recitation, and permissibly some or many in discussion. Only in discussion may there be seen — yet not of necessity must there be seen — a student following a student in turn; a student addressing a student; a student referring to a student's contribution; and a student evaluating a student's contribution. In recitation there will be no S–S or S–T turns but only T–S; no S–S address but only S–T; no S–S reference but only S–T; no S–S evaluation but only T–S. In discussion there may be some or many S–S turns; S–S as well as S–T address; S–S reference even in a T–S turn; and S–S evaluation, even S–T evaluation.

For example, in this discussion there are student sequences involving S–T and S–S as well as T–S evaluations, ending with the teacher's reversal of his position.

S1 — 'Cause X was more dominant, I guess.
T — Y was more dominant.
S2 — Uh-uh. X was.
S3 — X didn't know the other two.
S4 — But X was still more dominant than the other two.
T — Was not Y the extrovert?
SS — [—]
T — So, X the quiet introvert, was the most dominant. OK, now we're back to the question: . . .

Other examples appear in Mr T's history discussion. After Mr T disagrees with Barb ('I don't know if I totally agree with that'), Marty disagrees with both, and Sean disagrees with Marty:

Marty: I don't really disagree with Barb, but . . .
Sean: I think Marty was wrong, because . . .

Mr T then tells Marty that Sean is disagreeing and Marty agrees and disagrees: 'Yeah, well — No, he brought up a good point. But I mean . . .' Then Julie speaks, referring to previous student contributions ('Remember we were saying that about why . . .'); Diane disagrees with Julie, and Mark agrees with Diane:

Diane: Well, I don't know. Like, . . .
Mark: She's got a good point . . .

None of this kind of talk will be heard in a recitation. There is evaluation aplenty but not in terms of agree/disagree and not by students, much less of the teacher. Evaluation is always by the teacher, in terms of rightness of student answer. That is partly because of the teacher-student question-answer exchange, and partly because nothing much is in question.

Here are examples of other student sequences in addition to evaluation — student-student turns, address, and reference.

1. 'Barb, what do you think of narcs?' (also a student question, and a student-student question)
2. 'That — something like that I think is good, too, because . . .' (the previous student had said that it was good)
3. a. 'And my mother, she says, "Look, . . ."'
   b. 'My mother — it's no big deal. I'll . . .'
4. a. 'I don't see what Paul and Steve said as two separate ideas . . .'
   b. 'I agree with her almost all the way up until the end, where she said . . .'
   c. 'I think he has a point of view or whatever, but I think, taking from what Christine said, that . . . And just like he said, . . .'

In a discussion students speak in student sequences (turns, address, reference, evaluation), amidst an unpredictable mix of speakers and moves in optional cycles involving a mix of exchanges, because together and individually they are trying to understand or resolve something in their minds or hearts. And that is because something is *at issue* in a discussion — a question. On that point there turns a signal difference between recitation and discussion.

Characteristic questions

The most distinctive feature of questions during discussion is that they are open for discussion rather than closed for answer. Although there are many questions in a recitation very little is in question, other than whether the student can supply the right answer. In discussion, the very thing that is being asked is actually what is in question. Ordinarily the questioner does not know the answer and neither, in a sense, does the respondent: they arrive at some answer rather than recite the answer that both know beforehand. Thus an easy way to discern a discussion question is to look at the answer.

The source of the answer does not lie in the teacher, text, lesson, or assignment; the content of the answer is not predetermined, and its rightness is not foreordained. There may or may not exist a 'right' answer; there is at least more than one answer that is right, or several acceptable ones; the teacher (or text) may or may not have an answer that is right; the student is to get some right or useful answer (rather than the one right answer); and there may be different right answers for various students (rather than one and the same right answer for all students). All of these features can most easily be seen in the way that answers are handled once they are given.

In a recitation answers are treated as if there were but one right one, and that one already known to the teacher who, it seems, is seeking to discover whether the student can supply that answer which is right. After the answer is given, the teacher evaluates it by saying 'right' or not, often repeating the right answer. After an answer to a discussion question, the teacher will not say right, ordinarily, but may say 'Good!' This evaluation refers not so much to the content of the answer as to the quality of the move of answering. 'Good. OK, good. I think that's, you know, a really clear analysis.' (vs. 'Right, OK, that's a really correct answer.') 'OK, good. That wasn't in the book either.' (vs. 'OK, right. That's just what your book said.')

Rather than 'right/wrong' plus repeat of right answer or repeat of question, in discussion the generic response is 'agree/disagree' plus reference to answer, followed by self's contribution. Students might say 'I don't really disagree with Barb, but you know . . .' or 'She's got a good point' or 'I think he has a point of view or whatever, but I think . . .'. Teachers might say 'OK. And yet, you know, as Regina was saying, . . .' or 'OK, I can see where you're coming from, but I don't know if I totally agree with that.' Yet the teacher may make no such evaluative move at all but only some acknowledgement of the answer, perhaps even 'Thank you.' Or the teacher might pass directly to a second student.

When in a recitation the teacher moves directly to a second student, the move betokens that the first answer was incorrect; students will continue to offer answers serially until one is confirmed and a further question is asked. Meantime the original question may be repeated.

What is nationalism?
— X.
All right, but what is it?
— Y.
Yeah, but what is it, basically? What is it?
— It's a Z.
All right, it's a Z. OK. It's a Z. OK.

(If the teacher moves directly to a second *question*, the move betokens that the first answer was correct.) Such a move in a discussion does not betoken rejection of the first answer, nor confirmation of it, but a turn to other acceptable answers to the same question.

The turn to a second student, the treatment of the first answer, and the character of answer itself all point to the distinctive status of questions during discussion. It follows that the teacher does well to practise a distinctive use of questions as appropriate to discussion.

USE OF QUESTIONS

Discussion calls for a special and sparse use of questions. Whereas dozens of questions and questioning techniques service recitation, only a special two are conducive to discussion — posing the single question for discussion, and asking the few questions that perplex self. Everyone in the room, students and teacher, is called on to use these questions; and all will have to learn to ask them.

Discussion question

Pose the question that is at issue for discussion. This is the single question to which the discussion as a whole represents an answer or an effort to address. A single question is sufficient for an hour's discussion. But to conceive of that question will require thought; to formulate it requires labor; and to pose it, tact.

The teacher's first act is not to ask the question but to think about which question to ask. Long before class starts, you devote yourself to pondering the issue that will serve purpose and circumstance. For example, you wonder about which matter follows from previous class activity, captures the students' present predicament, and promises to advance the class once that issue has been discussed.

127

Figure 5.1: Pedagogy of discussion questions

Prepare the Question for Discussion

1. Conceive of just the right one.
2. Formulate it in just the right way.
3. Pose just that one in just that way.

Ask Questions that Perplex Self

(Do not ask questions that do not perplex self.)

Use Alternatives to Questioning

1. *Statements* — State your selected thought in relation to what the student has just said.
2. *Student Questions* — Provide that a student ask a question related to what the speaker has just said.
3. *Signals* — Signal your reception of what the student is saying, without yourself taking or holding the floor.
4. *Silences* — Say nothing at all but maintain a deliberate, appreciative silence for three seconds or so, until the original speaker resumes or another student enters in.

Your next act is not to ask the question but to formulate it for the asking. Long before class starts you write the question out on a piece of paper. You immediately discover that not one but several questions come to mind about the matter that you have selected for discussion; whereupon you are faced with selecting that one which shall be the question for discussion. This is the question that you now start to write out on a piece of paper. You then discover that not one but several versions of that question start from the pen; whereupon you are faced with selecting that one which shall formulate the selected question for discussion. You laboriously write that question out until satisfied that the sentence before you expresses the issue that you have in mind (you may in the process be changing your mind for the better), in such a way as to provide for a range of alternative, competing answers or otherwise fruitful contributions to discussion. Thus, what had appeared to be a simple question hardly calling for the trouble of writing turns out to be a laborious matter needing to be written down before you can even know what the question is.

Last is the classroom act of posing the question for discussion. You might write it on the blackboard for all to see and later to refer to. You will need only a few remarks to present the question, for you have already taken the trouble to see that it is just the question that makes sense to discuss, given the previous class activity, the students' present predicament, and your purpose. In your few introductory remarks, you take disciplined care not to pose any other questions while posing that number one question (e.g., 'In other words, Q2' or 'I mean, Q3' or 'You know, how about Q4'). You have already faced the other questions and you know they are not the question for discussion. After presenting the question, discussion might begin with a few rounds of analyzing rather than addressing it, until the question makes to the students the same sense it makes to you.

Of course, there is a far easier way to proceed. You show up at the start of class and ask the question that occurs to you, letting discussion take its own course. After a few students have spoken you can ask the other question that occurs to you. A bit later you can clarify the question you meant to ask but that students are not addressing. Then you ask a few related questions that are circling about the issue, or leading up to it or following from it, plus a couple of questions about interesting side points and maybe a series of questions pursuing some point that arises in answer to some question that has been asked. In that way the discussion will hit all possible points and everyone will have said at least something about something. At the end you can conclude by telling the students what the question for discussion is. 'OK. So the *real* question here, really, is not X or Y as we were saying, but Z. OK, tomorrow we'll . . .' The alternative is to pose the question for discussion at the start of discussion. That will require conceiving it and formulating it well before the start.

In addition to posing the question at the start, the question may be identified at some midpoint or end of discussion. That is not to repeat the original question but to identify the question which now appears at issue, given what has transpired to that point. 'OK, good. So now we're left with the question, . . .' You have a good idea of what such questions might be because you have already sketched the various pieces, alternatives, and sequelae in the interrogative panoply as you labored to formulate the question for discussion.

A related practice is to identify the question that appears to underlie a series of contributions, perhaps in an effort to distinguish it from the question for discussion and to rally discussion around that. 'Well, the way I see what we've sorta been talking about here is, you know, Q2 or something, which is a little bit different, I think, from the main question we kinda started with on the board.' Students as well as teacher might well practice identifying these questions, especially when a student identifies the question that he believes himself to have been answering. Then you will know the question he is answering and he will know the question you are asking.

Even if you are a bit unsure of what you're doing when conducting a discussion, you can at least be sure of what you're asking. All that is involved is a single question. Conceive of just the right one beforehand, and formulate it in just the right way; then at the start of discussion pose just that one in just that way (see Figure 5.1).

Perplexity questions

Ask the questions that perplex self. Although there is but a single question for discussion, several individual questions may arise to your mind during the discussion; and although the discussion question may or may not bother you, these other questions actually perplex you. These are the questions to ask during a discussion.

The other side of this coin is not to ask questions that do not perplex self. Ask only those questions that perplex self. That may well be difficult to do, for many good reasons. In general, asking such questions is non-normative, especially in classrooms and especially by teachers.

As a teacher you may be used to asking questions that do not perplex you, and unaccustomed to asking those that perplex. You may be practised in asking questions that do not perplex students, in hopes of perplexing them. Students may have learned to presume that you or teachers are not perplexed when you ask a question, and to expect that teachers will not ask a question when perplexed. And students may have learned to ask just the kind of questions that you or teachers do.

Perplexity describes a well-defined experience of not knowing or understanding something and of needing and desiring to know it. (There are many things we don't know and don't care to know.) Ignorance, uncertainty, confusion and need are not states that a knowledgeable, authoritative, mature and self-sufficient personage like a teacher is either accustomed or expected to display. Nor will students readily make such a display of themselves in the public midst of peers. (The smart students know the answers; the others ask dumb questions.) But these are just the states that are commonly experienced, to some degree, during a discussion; and it is only in this state of perplexity that a question is rightly asked in discussion.

Students as well as teacher rightly ask questions that perplex self.

No examples can be given of such questions because they look like any other questions. But they sound and feel quite different, while the questioner too has a different look about him. Perplexity is an organismic experience felt and displayed in the lower reaches of the body as well as in the loftier cognitive recesses. It need not be a cataclysmic experience, only condign to the question — e.g., a slight but perceptible discomfort over a minor, fleeting matter: 'What time is it?' 'Do you know the way to San Jose?' Or some grand and pressing matter: 'How much more time do you give me, Doctor?' 'What is the way to happiness?' Or yet: 'Did the American colonists have the right to revolt against Britain?' 'How do they get rockets to the moon?' — and other perplexities piddling or ponderous about any subject-matter in school.

In asking about these and any other matters whatsoever, the perplexed self holds forth certain well-defined presumptions. He does not know the answer or is unsure of the answer he may know; at least it is *not* the case that he does know full well. He thinks that there is at least one true, direct and correct answer, but either doesn't have one or doesn't know which one, including the one he has, is correct. He needs and desires to have a satisfying answer. He believes that such an answer can be gotten, and he is willing to do what it takes to get one. He anticipates that the respondent or the world might well have the answer and can or will supply it if asked. Finally, he commits himself to the *truth of the question*, believing what the question says, the suppositions that lie behind it, the words and meanings it expresses, the world it projects, and so on. This manner of asking is only as serious as the truth and its consequences.

As an easy way of telling the truth in your own case, all you have to know is that you don't know the answer and that you need the 'information' or whatever in response. That is quite different from knowing the information and needing the student's answer. When you ask a recitation question you want to know the student's answer but not the information that constitutes the answer. When you ask a perplexity question you need to know the answer itself, and perhaps not one will be able to give it to you. Therefore, perplexity questions may be posed aloud in wonderment, as well as asked of some student who appears to know what you do not know and need to know. In that same way, students too can well ask the questions that perplex them.

Discussion then ensues as people join in inquiry over perplexing matters that they are attempting to know, understand, adapt or resolve for themselves. Failing that, recitation ensues as people exchange answers with other people who also already know them.

Discussion does not proceed by question-answer. The teacher poses only a single question for discussion, together with the few perplexing questions that might arise to his mind. A multitude of other questions may come to the lips of the practised teacher, perhaps one question at every juncture in the talk. That is how recitation proceeds. But these questions are better left unasked in discussion for their failure to be genuinely perplexing to self, and for fear of foiling the discussion and turning it into a recitation. Instead, in favor of discussion, the teacher chooses to use alternatives to questioning. Only when self is perplexed does a question become the alternative of choice.

USE OF ALTERNATIVES

At the juncture where a student has just finished speaking, as in response to a question, the teacher has the choice of asking a question or using an alternative, non-questioning technique. The choice is made in favor of that action which promises to serve pedagogical purpose in this classroom circumstance. In general, for purposes of discussion the use of alternatives is more promising than asking questions.

Four kinds of alternatives are available for the choosing, and any number of specific ones — statements, student questions, signals, and silences. Instead of asking a question, the teacher can choose to:

1. make a *statement* of his selected thought in relation to what the student has just said; or
2. provide for a *student question* related to the speaker's contribution; or
3. give some *signal* of receiving what the speaker has said, without himself taking and holding the floor; or yet
4. say nothing at all but maintain a deliberate, appreciative *silence*.

Each of these kinds of alternatives promises to serve broad pedagogical purpose by stimulating student thought and response, by fostering discussion, and by teaching students appropriate discussion behaviors.

As for specific alternatives, these are set out in Figure 5.2, listed

Figure 5.2: Alternatives to questioning

Alternative		Generic Example	A Counterexample
Statements			
1. *Declarative statement* State the (pre-question) thought that occurs to you as a result of what the speaker has just been saying.	S T	– X is the case. [thinking Y] – Y is the case.	Any post-thought question, e.g., What other letter is the case?
2. *Reflective restatement* State your understanding of what the speaker has just said. (a) Repeat it	S T	– X is the case. – X is the case.	What do you mean?
(b) Summarize or characterize it	S	– A, B, Q, H, O, V, G, C, J, M, A, T and Z is the case.	Do you mean X? Do you mean Y? What are you trying to say?
	T	– The alphabet is the case, or maybe some jumble of letters.	
3. *Statement of mind* Describe in truth your state of mind, and none other, in relation to what the speaker has just been saying.	S T	– X is the case. [mind is square] – My mind is square about what you're saying.	What do the rest of you in here think about what S just said?
4. *Statement of interest* State whatever it is that you are interested in hearing further about what the speaker has just been saying.	S T	– X in the case [interested in Y about X] – I'm interested in hearing Y about X.	Why do you think X? What are some aspects of X?

Figure 5.2 *contd.*

5. *Student referral*
State the relation between what the speaker has just said and what a previous speaker has said.

S1 — X is the case.
S2 — Anti-X is the case.
T — So you're saying anti-X and S1 is saying X, the opposite.

How does that relate to what S1 said?

6. *Teacher reddition*
Give an account of your own status (knowledge, experience, feeling) regarding the matter at hand.

S — X is the case with me.
T — With me, the case is . . .

And what's the case with you, S2?

Student Questions

S1 — Something is the case, I don't know.

7. *Speaker's question*
Provide that the speaker formulate a question about what he is struggling to think and say.

T — Relax for a minute and think up the question that's still bothering you about that.

What exactly do you think the case is?

8. *Class question*
Provide that another student pose a question about the speaker's contribution or the matter under discussion.

— Let's take a minute to hear the question that somebody else might be thinking of about that.

Anybody else? What is the case here?

9. *Discussion question*
Provide that students formulate the question that now appears at issue in the discussion.

— Maybe it's time now to hear a few suggestions as to the kind of question we should be asking now, given everything that's been said up to this point.

Let's move on to the next question: What is the case over there?

S1 or 2 — Is X the case?
T — You're wondering if X is the case. Good question.

Any answer, e.g., Yes/no.
Any counterquestion, e.g. Well what do *you* think? — Is X the case?

Signals

10. *Phatics*
Uttering a brief phrase, quietly exclaim feeling in reaction to what the speaker has just finished saying.

S1 — X is the case
T [phatic] — Oh, X is nice.
  [filler] — Mm-hmm.

Any question.

11. *Fillers*
Emitting some word or sound, indicate attentive interest in what the speaker has said or is in process of saying.

S1 — And Y is the case, too.

12. *Pass*
By gesture or statement, pass the next turn at talk to another speaker.

S1 — X is the case.
T [pass] Yes, S2.
S2 — Y is the case.

Silences

13. *Deliberate silence*
Say nothing at all but maintain a deliberate, appreciative silence (for 3–5 secs) until the original speaker resumes or another speaker enters in.

S1 — X is the case.
T [rehearses in mind: 'Baa, baa, black sheep, Have you any wool?']
S1 — And Y, too, come to think about it.

Any question is counterexample . . . while rehearsing in mind: — nod, nod, does S1 have any more?

Figure 5.2 *contd.*

	T	['Yes sir, yes sir, Three bags full.']
	S1 or 2 — But not Z.	
	T	'One for my master, One for my dame, One for the little boy Who lives in the lane.']
	S2 or 1 — Z isn't the case because . . .	
14. *Non-deliberate silence* You'd better figure out something to do. If in trouble, start asking questions.	S1 — X is the case. [confusion, trouble]	— nod, nod, hold for 3 seconds!
		— look at speaker
	T — Question.	— look at a girl
	S2 — Answer.	— look at a boy
	T — Question.	— look down the back row.
	S3 — Answer.	
		Discussion is counterexample. Class is now in Recitation mode.

by type — various statements, student questions, signals, silences. For each alternative Figure 5.2 gives the definition, the generic example, and a counterexample (viz., a question). Here in the text we will follow the handy scheme in Figure 5.2, adding detail and commentary, the rationale for using the given alternative, suggestions for learning to use it, and examples of its use in actual classroom discussions.

Statements

Instead of asking a question, *state your selected thought in relation to what the student has said*. Contrary to what might be obvious, people do respond to statements. And student responses to teacher statements promise to be longer and more complex than their answers to questions.

Any number of thoughts can be stated, and various kinds of statements made of them. The principle is to make a straightforward statement of thought disciplined by pedagogical purpose in this classroom circumstance. Six kinds of statements that serve to purpose are identified in Figure 5.2. When a student has just made a contribution, you can choose to make a declarative statement or a reflective restatement, state your mind or your interest, make a student referral or give a teacher reddition. The first two of these will be treated at greater length so as to clarify the scheme in Figure 5.2 and to establish the rationale for using other alternatives of this type.

1. Declarative statement: State the (pre-question) thought that occurs to you as a result of what the student has just been saying

For example (Figure 5.2), the student has just said that something is the case: 'X is the case'. The thought occurs to the teacher that Y is the case. So he says to the student: 'Y is the case.' For a counterexample, instead of stating that Y is the case the teacher *asks* the student, 'What other letter is the case?'

That is the *generic* example — the one example that describes all of the specific, individually different examples that can be thought of. Accordingly, the student doesn't actually say the very words, 'Something (or X) is the case,' and the teacher doesn't actually say back, 'Y is the case.' Nor is it an argument. The student is stating his thought and the teacher is stating his related thought; the thoughts can be complementary as well as opposed. Here is a general example and counterexample.

The student has just said something, as in answer to a question. Whenever the student says something, he is stating that something is the case — X. 'Roses are red.' That's X. While the student is speaking, you the teacher are thinking something in relation to that (among many other thoughts occurring to you at the moment). You too are thinking that something is the case. 'Violets are blue.' That's Y. 'You look like a monkey that lives in the zoo.' That's Z. You do not state your thought Z because it offers less promise of serving pedagogical purpose in this circumstance. Instead you state your *selected* thought, Y, in relation to the student's contribution X. Your 'Violets are blue' complements the student's 'Roses are red,' and there you have, the two of you, a nice couplet.

Any counterexample to this alternative is, naturally, a teacher question. The student has said that X is the case (Roses are red). You are thinking Y (Violets are blue). Instead of stating Y you *ask* the student, 'What other letter is the case?' (What color are violets? What flowers are blue?) The student has just told you what letter he thinks is the case. You've just told him that you will not tell him what letter you think is the case but that he must tell you what letter you think the case is. So he says A. You say no and ask what other letter is the case. He says B. You say no, think hard, and you ask what other letter is the case. Eventually he or someone else will come to say Y and mercifully you will say yes and state that Y is the case. The alternative is to state at the outset that Y is the case. Then the student has the benefit of your thought in relation to his thought, and now discussion of two related thoughts can proceed forthwith.

Before explaining the obvious benefit of stating your thought in relation to the student's thought, let us see it in another general example. A student, Gloria, is talking about the cost of tea in India. You, the teacher, are thinking 'We don't import any tea from India, we get all of our tea from China.' You state that thought. Gloria is informed by that statement, corrects her understanding and works the new intelligence into her thinking about tea and/or about India, next bespeaking her revised thought on that. Or Gloria is not informed by your statement, having already known that fact, and she so informs you, adding the intelligence that the point she was trying to make or leading up to by discoursing on tea in India was — such and such, which has nothing to do with the price of tea in China. Now you are informed of Gloria's point, you have corrected your own previous misunderstanding, and you can next follow Gloria more closely. Discussion has advanced and the two of you are in pursuit, each accommodating to the other's thought. The alternative is for you to derail Gloria's thinking and rout discussion by asking her, 'How much tea do we import from India?' or 'Where do we get most of our tea from, Gloria?' That way you will never know what Gloria's point was to have been; and Gloria may never know either, not having quite discovered it yet before having to turn away from her thinking and attend to your question in search of your veiled thought.

Here are ten specific examples drawn from recordings of actual classroom discussion. In each case some student has just said something like 'X is the case.' Here is the teacher's statement of 'Y is the case,' together with a possible counterexample for the statement actually made by the teacher.

1. 'X certainly hasn't been the major reason behind Y.' — What has been the major reason behind Y?

2. 'Or even sometimes you see X along with Y. That sometimes happens too, I think.' — What letter sometimes goes along with Y? What else sometimes happens, do you think?

3. 'Well, OK, but see, they're not saying that because there's no X there's no Y, or Z.' — What are they really saying?

4. 'Now, that doesn't mean not-X. That just means you don't have to get Y.' — What does that mean?

5. 'Well, I'm not sure that's their basic argument. I don't think — I think the basic argument is just the fact that they're X.' — What is their basic argument?

6. 'Well, X — first of all, X is not located in Y.' — Where is X located? What is located in Y?

7. 'Well, I mean, it's just like anything else, part of the reason for X, though, is because of Y.' — What is the reason for X? What role does Y play?

8. 'OK, I think that there is a difference, that X does this whereas Y does that.' — Is there a difference between X and Y? How do X and Y compare in what they do?

9. 'I don't think they're   — Do you think X and Y are
   totally incompatible, the   incompatible? What other
   things you're saying, X   way is there of looking at
   and Y. I just think there   X and Y?
   are two different ways of
   looking at them.'
10. 'That's a little bit unfair, I — Is that fair, would you
    would say.'   say?

It should be clear that any statement at all, any thought can be declared, as simple as '2 + 2 = 4'. That is why specific examples can be misleading. These examples were selected to show some of the more obvious ways of stating 'corrective' and complementary kinds of thoughts. But the thoughts need not be corrective or anything else, only *informative* of the teacher's thought in relation to the student's contribution. 'Roses are red.' — 'Violets are blue.'

Yet why on earth would a student *respond* to some statement like 'Violets are blue'?

In the first place it should be noted that 'Violets are blue' does not come out of the blue but is related to the student's previously-expressed thought.

A second general reason that students will respond to your statements, even when unrelated to their thought, is for the pressing fact that you are the teacher, and students must respond to things that the teacher says to them. This social constraint also operates in other circumstances involving superiors and subordinates, and it further operates in some everyday encounters between apparent peers. Just try it out. Try not to respond to a statement addressed to you by a friend, or yet by a stranger, in some harmless circumstance, say in a bar or standing in line for a bus or for a cashier in a store. Only Steve McQueen and Clint Eastwood can get away with ignoring the statement (and of course they would never be caught standing in line for anything). The rest of us will hear something like, 'Hey, I'm *talking* to *you*!' — and the circumstance rapidly begins to threaten. Polite response helps keep out of harm's way. Thus will students respond to our statements. Steve McQueen won't, but that is why he is in the movies, having for that reason been kicked out of school. The rest of us stay in by responding to things that teachers say, like 'Violets are blue.' We even write them down.

But students will not merely respond. They respond at some length and complexity to relevant teacher statements. And their responses to statements can be expected to be longer and more complex than answers to questions. By contrast to questions of any type, statements are more *open* in response-initiative, content (including topic), process and duration; they are in *direct* relation to what the student has just said; they are more *informative*, supplying information and intelligence, more likely unknown to the student and certainly unknown to him as being our thought in relation to his. Finally, the statement requires *accommodation*. The information that it supplies must be accommodated in relation to the student's expressed thought. In accepting or rejecting the information, the student makes some adjustment of the complex of his knowledge and thinking about the subject; and in making that adjustment and speaking that accept/reject, he will first have to examine and construe that statement, elaborate and explain his accept/reject, evaluate and justify, illustrate or give counterexamples, ponder and wonder, etc. That is more complex thought as well as more lengthy talk. And that is the kind of 'higher-cognitive' response that students give even to 'lower-cognitive' kinds of statements, for even a simple mere fact can disorganize a made-up mind.

To use this alternative requires first that we deliberately break the connection between a question and the thought that precedes it. ('State the pre-question thought.') Before the question comes to our lips a thought has occurred to our mind. With teachers especially, this connection seems automatic and nearly instantaneous. We have a fleeting thought and immediately form a question to ask. This connection must be broken and the thought spoken.

It takes effort to break the connection, and practised effort actually to speak the thought instead of the question. The question comes so readily to the lips and rolls off the tongue. In part that is because we may think that questions are the proper thing for a teacher to speak. Teachers commonly speak in questions and questions are commonly thought to get students to think and respond, to keep a discussion going. Few people seem to observe that teacher statements get students to think and respond, and foster discussion. In other part that is because we may not know what else to speak at that moment, yet we have to speak and we have to get students to respond. The alternative of making a declarative statement instructs us as to what else to do, it satisfies the need to speak and it gets students to respond. But there is a third part to the effortlessness of questions. That is the fact that we pay little attention to the thought that precedes a question in our mind, and we leave it without much formulation. So it is hard to state the thought; we go right to the question.

The connection between pre-question thought and question has to be broken, the question stayed, and the thought attended to, formulated, and then enunciated. You can learn to do that, as I did, by being analytical and introspective, catching yourself in a question and then looking for the prior thought; and by deliberately practising and disciplining yourself to formulate and state that thought. But I have invented an easier way for you to learn this alternative, especially if you are a beginner.

All you have to do is to *answer your own question aloud*. Don't ask it, just give the answer. That way you will not have to be analytical about it, searching your mind for connections among thoughts fleeting about in the dark recesses. And you won't have to put a disciplined stop to the process while you formulate the thought, all the while standing in front of the class looking like you don't know what you are doing. Take the question that so quickly comes to mind and go right ahead and answer it.

For example, Hernandez says 'Roses are red.' You say 'Violets, Hernandez — violets are blue'; or 'Blue, Hernandez — some flowers are blue, like violets.' Which version you speak depends on your question: 'What flowers are blue?' 'What color are violets?' Similarly, when Gloria is going on about the price of tea in India, you say 'No tea, Gloria —- we don't import any tea from India' (How much tea do we import from India?); or, 'China, Gloria, not India — China is where we get our tea from nowadays' (Where do we get our tea from?). And when LeRoy is trying to prove his point by citing employment rates in the 1930s, you merely say 'But when the war broke out, LeRoy, unemployment dropped' (What happens to unemployment in time of war? What causes a drop in unemployment?).

The way to learn this alternative may be to answer your own questions instead of asking them. It also helps to be a beginning teacher, so that you can get it right from the start. But the key to the alternative is to give the student the benefit of your thought. Using a declarative statement, state the selected thought that occurs to you as a result of what the student has just said.

2. Reflective restatement: State your understanding of what the speaker has just said, giving your sense of it in one economical and exact sentence

There are two basic ways to restate the student's contribution (Figure 5.2).

(a) *Repeat it*. The student says 'X is the case.' You say 'X is the case.' As a counterexample, you *ask* 'What do you mean?'

(b) *Summarize or characterize it*. The student speaks various letters from A to Z, in some jumbled order. You say 'The alphabet is the case, or maybe some jumble of letters.' As a counterexample, you ask 'Do you mean X? Do you mean Y? What are you trying to say?'

To this alternative the student will respond with something like 'Right' or 'Well, what I meant was —'. In either case he will almost invariably go on to discourse at greater length and with richer thought on the matter, enhancing his original response by extending and improving it. Even when you do no more than to repeat the student's 'Roses are red,' the response will likely be 'Right, and violets are blue.' In this case it is the student who forms the nice couplet, completing and enriching his original contribution.

Here from actual classroom recordings are some examples of reflective restatements, showing what they can look like and how students have responded to them.

In Mr T's lesson on European history, Diane is speaking about Louis XIV's reasons for persecuting the Huguenots, and the teacher characterizes her contribution.

> T: So you feel that he was justified in what he was doing, as far as he was concerned — he could justify it to himself.
> S: Yeah, he could justify it to himself. But then, . . . (continues for eleven seconds).

In a sensitive discussion about sexual topics in the students' home life, Marilyn is speaking about her family's way of talking about sex. The teacher reflects her statement and she elaborates, connecting her contributions with a previous student's.

> T: You do this all together.
> S: Yeah, my mother and father and all the rest of us. And just like he said, . . . (continues for 21 seconds).

George then speaks about his case. 'See, and in my case . . .' The teacher summarizes and George expresses a shorter but more emotive contribution (as appropriate to the subject and purpose of this discussion).

> T: She won't listen.
> S: Right. So I feel, I get angry with her, you know. (five seconds)

143

Other reflective restatements used by this teacher begin with the phrase, 'So you're saying that . . .' For example, 'So you're saying that your parents never sat you down and talked about sex.'

In using this alternative you might find it helpful to begin with some introductory phrase making it plain to yourself as well as to the student that you are trying to make a restatement rather than your own statement or interpretation. For example:

— So, you feel/think that . . .
— So, you're saying that . . .
— I get from what you say that . . .
— Oh, in your mind, the . . .
— So what you're talking about is . . .
— You think/mean, in other words, that . . .

But these are mere preliminaries, and they are not even necessary. The essence of this alternative is what you say *after* such an introduction.

What you say is your understanding of what the student has said. It is no easy matter to catch someone's sense and then render it in just the right few words. That is harder still to do in a classroom discussion, where people who don't quite know what they think and who aren't good at expressing what they think, are telling you what they think. For these very reasons they are in school and the class is a discussion; and for the same reasons you the teacher can choose to use this alternative. It is even hard just to repeat what someone has said, and, in repeating it, to convey just the sense that the speaker had in saying it to begin with — the correct twist, the right tone, the same measure of certainty, and so forth. You cannot even begin to do any of this if you have not disciplined yourself to listen to the student in the first place.

First you must attend to the student, listening to what he is saying. Second, you must intend to understand the student, listening for what he is meaning and for the way in which he is meaning it. Then you make the reflective restatement, giving your understanding of what the student's understanding is. By contrast, most people will give their understanding of the point at issue, substituting theirs for the other speaker's understanding. Most listeners do not intend to grasp the speaker's meaning as the speaker would have it but as they would construe it. Finally, many people do not even listen to what is being said but spend the waiting time getting ready for their next turn at talk — formulating questions, objections, corrections, positions, tangents. Then in their turn they base their move on their imaginary construction of the previous speaker's words and meanings. 'Yeah, I know what you mean' — followed by a demonstration that they have no idea of your meaning.

In such a case it seems polite enough to ask the other person 'What do you mean?' But it is pointless to ask. For, he has just told you what he means. Furthermore he has no idea of what to say in answer, other than to repeat or to reword that which he has already said and which you have ignored or dismissed in the first place. Hence to be polite but not boring he will customarily answer by saying something *different* from what he had said; and you, rather than impolitely asking once again what he means, may choose to accept the second, novel contribution as merely a version of the first. The alternative is to inform him at the outset of what you understand him to have meant. Then he can know which part of his meaning to clarify or reaffirm, etc.

Above all the speaker is motivated to make that attempt because you seem *interested* in understanding what he means before you go on to give your own meaning. In that way real rather than imagined meanings, and shared rather than private ones, come to form the basis of your discussion.

A reflective restatement signals to everyone in the room the importance of attending and listening to what someone is saying, before reacting to it. And it demonstrates before everyone's eyes the amazing difficulty of appreciating it rightly. We commonly misconstrue the meaning and often enough mishear the words. It is hard to get things straight. The proof is when you try this alternative for the first 100 times or so, only to discover that you don't know what the speaker is talking about. Time and again he responds with some such phrase as 'Well, what I meant to say was . . .', if not 'No, that's not what I meant at all.' But that negative response is a fruitful one, as fruitful as a 'Yes, that's just exactly what I meant!' For the restatement gives the speaker an opportunity, invariably taken, to clarify, elaborate, and establish his meaning, sometimes discovering it for himself only on the second time around.

A reflective restatement permits the speaker (and other students) to infer, rightly, that what he thinks and says *matters* some. It confirms the speaker in his effort to contribute. It helps him to express thoughts gradually more clearly and fully. It assures him of understanding. And it makes a public possession of a private meaning. The result is to encourage participation, both speaking and listening, and to facilitate relevant discussion of actual rather than imaginary meanings. Along the way it also teaches appropriate discussion behavior. After a time, the teacher can invite students to try this alternative themselves.

The key to this alternative is to make the very try at it. Beginners can do it effectively, even when they don't quite get the speaker's meaning right or don't state it in just the right words. To do *that* takes a master. But you don't have to be a master to use this alternative. All you have to do is to state your understanding of what the student has said. Your understanding may be wrong but your use of the alternative right.

3. Statement of mind: Describe in truth your state of mind, and none other, in relation to what the speaker has just been saying

A student has said that X is the case. Your mind is in some state, let us say it is square. You so inform the student: 'My mind is square about what you're saying.' Then the student knows your state of mind and responds directly to it. A counterexample is to ask, 'What do the rest of you in here think about what he's just said?' That way no student will know your state of mind. You will not reveal it, although they are to reveal theirs.

During a discussion the teacher can experience any number of states of mind and use various ways to state them. All the variety is of no concern. The key is to describe the state of your mind, and none other.

One of the most common states of mind during a discussion is to be *unclear* or *confused* about what the student is saying. You so inform him: 'My mind is unclear about what you're saying', 'I'm confused about what you're saying.' In this state you want to respond but you don't have anything clear to say, so you describe your state of mind.

— I'm not sure I understand, exactly.
— I don't quite follow you there.
— I'm afraid I'm just not getting your point.
— I must be missing something about what you say.

Of course, there is no use tip-toeing around with such delicacies of phrase if they do not in truth describe your state of mind.

For goodness' sake, don't say 'I'm afraid I'm not quite getting your point' when in truth you have it nailed down and object to it. Say rather 'I object to what you are saying,' and then state your preferred point. 'I don't agree with you there, because an X is a Y.'

But if in truth you don't understand, state that which you do not understand. 'Ah, Willie, what I don't understand is your saying, "I'm not knocking it, but it's stupid." ' If you are confused, state your confusion; if opposed, state your opposition. If you understand and disagree, say so: 'OK, I can see where you're coming from, but I don't know if I can totally agree with that.' On the other hand, if you are agreeable, state your agreement: 'OK, I'll go along with that.' If surprised, state your surprise: 'I'm surprised that you feel X. Somehow in my mind you'd think it'd be kinda Y, in some way.' All of that is to describe in truth the state of your mind, and none other.

During a discussion it commonly happens to me that I am in a *lost state*. I find myself at a loss witnessing exchanges between people with no trace of understanding anymore the connection between them. This is not a fruitful state to be in either as pedagogue or participant. Then one of the students starts talking at length to me! Although I understand the words, I can't construe the speech for lack of understanding its purpose and relevance. So I say something like: 'I know that you're saying something important to me but I'm not getting the connection between what you're saying and what she just said.' In response the student commonly informs me that he is saying X because she has said Y — whereupon *she* commonly remarks 'But I meant Z,' and he says 'Oh.' Now I understand, and so does he and she. We three are back on track, together, and I discover from scattered murmurings that other people in the room have also only now found themselves following along. Great minds may run in the same channels, but I find it hard to keep track of a discussion.

A statement of mind enhances the discussion itself and also teaches students appropriate discussion behavior. First, it informs the person who is speaking to you of your state of mind, and it evokes the speaker's response to your exact state. Second, it gets you back into the swing of things, and other people too. Third, it establishes norms of responsible participation, such as the norm of speaking the truth of your mind and not bespeaking something else. It is a demonstration *against* the norms of sitting there and pretending that you get the gist of things; of listening to people while ignoring their meaning; of speaking back and forth without having any idea of what is being exchanged. These are the norms that make of 'discussion' a series of alternating monologues.

Two other states that I am frequently in during discussion are distraction and muddle. When in a *distracted state* I say: 'I'm sorry, I'm distracted right now' or 'I was thinking about something else

147

just then.' In response, the student can make another try at his point or he can seek to discover that supposedly more absorbing point that was preoccupying me. When in a *muddled state*, I say things like: 'Something about X bothers me, I don't know'; 'I'm trying to decide if X or Y is the case here'; 'I was just wondering whether X would make any difference.' Those sound very much like questions, but in this muddled state I am in no condition to ask a question, nor do I want to. I'm engaged in muddling through for the moment and a question to the student would neither communicate to him my state of mind nor get from him the kind of response I want. So I describe my state of mind and he responds to that.

When on the other hand I am in a *perplexed state* — when I don't know and I need and desire to know, and when I want help with knowing and I believe the student(s) can give that help — then I ask a question. That becomes the alternative of choice at that juncture.

4. Statement of interest: State whatever it is that you are interested in hearing further about what the speaker has just been saying

A student says that X is the case. You are interested in Y about X. You say: 'I'm interested in hearing Y about X.' A counterexample is to ask 'What are some aspects of X?' or worse, 'What about Y?'

This alternative is simplicity itself but strangely difficult for teachers to do. If you would like to hear more of the students' views on X, say: 'I'd like to hear more of your views on X.' That is an invitation to elaborate, somewhat more inviting than 'Elaborate on that' or 'What else do you think about X?'. 'Roses are red' — 'That's interesting, I'd like to hear more of your views on that' — 'Well, violets are blue.'

Here are some things that teachers are interested in but do not state their interest in, rather putting a question or directive about them. To state the interest requires both straightforwardness of thinking and some delicateness of phrasing.

Definition. 'I notice you keep stressing X, and I'd be interested in your definition of X.'

Example. 'It would help me to understand better if I had an example of X.'

Reasons/applications. 'I'm interested in knowing the reasons behind/uses of X.'

Objection. 'I'd like to learn the objection you have to X.'

Background. 'I think it'd really be interesting to hear about your background thinking/experience with X.'

Of course, if you are not interested in these things there is no use in stating your interest in them. This alternative is useful only when you choose to reveal your interest, and to reveal it in a direct and enticing way. You can choose other things to do when you are not interested or prefer to veil your interest.

For example, if you think the student has no good reason for saying X, you might ask him, 'Why do you think [something stupid like] X is the case?' A naive student will respond by haplessly giving you his reasons for thinking X, whereupon you demolish them in front of his face and everyone else's. A smart student will hide his reasons. You are not interested in his reasons, you know they are no good. You have some objection or correction to supply to his way of thinking about X, so you might usefully choose to state it, e.g., using a declarative statement to communicate the thought that has occurred to you as a result of what he has said. It makes no pedagogical sense either to ask for his reasons *or* to state an interest in them.

5. *Student referral: State the relation between what the speaker has just said and what a previous speaker has said, referring one student to another*

Student One has said that X is the case. Later Student Two says that anti-X is the case. You say to Student Two: 'So you're saying anti-X and Student One is saying X, the opposite.' As a counterexample you ask Student Two, 'How does that relate to what Student One said?' — asking her to state the relation that you perceive but will not tell her until she tells you first what relation you perceive. You prove that by saying no to the relation that she perceives. She answers your question: 'Well, I dunno, he was saying, you know, kinda the same thing, I think.' — 'He was saying the exact *opposite* of what you said!'

The alternative is to state the relation you see. Then the two students can look at each other, examine their contributions for any relation, and discuss the relations they might begin to have. 'Roses are red,' said he; 'Violets are blue,' says she; 'You form a couple, he and you,' says the romantically poetic teacher.

In Mr T's history discussion the teacher refers students to what Marty said, then refers Marty to what Sean says.

T: All right, Marty raised an interesting point just a few seconds ago. He said that X is the case.

Sean: I think Marty was wrong, because even though X, Y is still the case today.

T: All right, so he's totally disagreeing with what you had to say, Marty.

Marty: Yeah, well — No, he brought up a good point . . . But what I'm saying is . . .

The relations can describe complementarity as well as contradiction, similarity or inconsistency, and so on; and they can be stated in any number of ways. The variety is no matter. The point is to make a student referral. There seem to be three kinds of referral to make.

(a) *Refer speaker to student(s)*. 'I don't think Victor would go so far as to agree with you.' — 'OK. And yet, as Regina was saying, . . .'

(b) *Refer speaker to self*. 'Like you were saying, Pam, X is the case.' — 'All right, X is the case — going back to what you were saying earlier.'

(c) *Refer student(s) to speaker*. The Marty-students-Sean referrals are examples. Here is a more extensive referral: 'OK. I think, ah, we can go backwards to Marilyn's point and take off from that a bit. She said — and I think that some of you are agreeing with her — that X is the case. But Stacey said, and I think that Bonnie's saying the same thing, X is a case of Y.'

6. *Teacher reddition: Give an account of your own status (knowledge, experience, feeling) regarding the matter at hand*

Some student has just finished saying 'X is the case with me.' You say 'With me, the case is . . .' In response another student says 'That's the case with me, too' or 'See, and in my case . . .' A counterexample is to ask 'And what's the case with *you*, Student Two?' Student Two will respond but might not say what the case is with him — especially if the case is a touchy one and he has noticeably not been saying anything about it before.

In this discussion about a sensitive subject, sexual attitudes in homelife, the teacher is trying to induce students to speak about three topics, one of which is physical affection witnessed between their parents. At one point in an ongoing exchange with Larry, during which Larry is not speaking to that topic, the teacher directly asks him about it; Larry evades the question with a comment that produces nervous laughter from the class:

T: What about affection?

150

Larry: Yeah. I mean, it's not like I'd see my folks naked on the couch, no. (laughter)

So the teacher moves to give an account of the case with him. Larry then responds in kind, and so does Marilyn:

T: Right. So, quickly, one problem I know I have when I think about this question, I can't ever imagine my parents having sex, or whatever. But the thing is, you know, at least the kids — my parents had ten kids, so I know they went to bed together at least ten times, you know. (Laughter) You know, but I still have this trouble connecting that — the reality.

Larry: Yeah, I have that trouble too. I just couldn't — . . . (continues for eleven seconds).

Marilyn: In our family, you know, we have something like, . . . (continues for twelve seconds).

These are two responses, by students of different sexes, both responses on the topic, in the right manner, and at considerable length.

A point-for-point contrast to this fruitful development can be seen in two other classes discussing similar sensitive topics. In both classes a student has just stated the case with him/her, and the teacher asks a named student of the other sex (and other than the teacher's) what the case is with her/him. In both classes the student evades the question, the exchange stalls, and the teacher gives up — only to start doing it again with yet another student. Here first is Mr B and Nydia.

T: Nydia, do *you* agree with that?

S: What? I didn't hear —

T: What Leandro said, in terms of personal satisfaction being your goal, in sex?

S: I didn't hear what he said.

T: I just restated it.

S: Restate it again.

T: Would you like me to restate it again? He said, personal satisfaction in terms of being the goal in sex. Would you agree that would be your goal in entering into sexual relationships? Primarily for personal satisfaction?

S: I don't know.
T: You don't know what your goal would be, huh?
S: (no response, five seconds)
T: Gina?

The very same happens with Mrs K and Wally.

T: Wally, what do *you* think? Do you agree with her? That you can pretend?
S1: Pretend what?
T: Explain it again, please, Maryanne.
S2: You can pretend that you like being with this guy, but you really don't. You do it, you're just there.
S1: Just to pass one night, you're gonna tell him, just so you can — (laughter).
T: Would *you*, Sue?

In both of these classes the teacher has asked Student Two, 'And what's the case with *you*?' That didn't work with Student Two. So the teacher turned to do the same thing with Student Three. 'And what's the case with *you*?' An alternative move at either juncture would be teacher reddition: 'With me, the case is . . .' In response, as shown in the fruitful example, Student Two *and* Student Three, boy and girl, tell at length what the case is with them.

Teacher reddition is *an* alternative at this juncture. You don't have to use it. Furthermore, the topic does not have to be a sensitive one, and the reddition need not exhibit the teacher's personal feelings or intimate experiences. The topic can be a touchy or a stuffy one, the issue moral or intellectual, and the reddition an account of your knowledge, background, studies, feelings, and so on. This is a discussion, and *some* question is at issue.

Whatever the issue and whatever the reddition, an excellent way to start the reddition is to imitate the teacher in the first example: 'One problem I know I have when I think about this question . . .' Another teacher started this way: 'You know, the way I understand the problem is . . .' Here are other teachers giving redditions on various matters, academic and not.

— 'Well, I look at it like this. Nationalism is . . .' (history)
— 'I'm really very preoccupied with animals just now, because my friend and I, we have some cats, and . . .'(psychology)
— 'Oh, I know, I used to work in a store, too. And what

happened to me was . . . You find out how aware you are of other people talking about you, or just saying something.' (sociology)

In a 'U.S. Government' class discussing capital punishment, the teacher gave this poignant account of his experience, judgment, and decision on the matter at hand:

I mean, I've thought about killing a person before. I mean, you know, hate wells up inside you and you say, "I wish that person was dead." Now that's a sin, that's wrong. That's wrong to do. But we as sinful human beings get caught up in that kind of thing. But hopefully I am going to remain healthy enough where that I never carry that through to its fruition.

In another class there was no discussion of the subject-matter because the school had just revoked the students' smoking privileges, and the class had a heated discussion about that. At one point the teacher gave this reddition:

Well, you know — let me respond to that as somebody who is a smoker. You know, last year I smoked like a stuffed hog. And my wife and kids . . . And I quit in April . . . Because I know for a fact that I could pick up a cigarette right now and I could start puffing away.

Finally, in a senior class students are amazing the teacher with their opinions about getting married in a civil rather than religious ceremony, sparse rather than elaborate; and he gives this telling account of his status:

Well, that's good, I'm glad to hear some of these things. 'Cause, see, I've lived in my own little world here for so many years, and I don't run into a lot of people that would have a differing opinion from what I have. So that's why I always tell you people that you got about 30 good ideas in here against one of mine, and that's why I like to discuss things with you.

What a wonderful reddition for any teacher to give and any student to hear!

Student questions

Instead of asking a question, *provide that a student ask a question related to what the speaker has just said*. When well-provided for, student questions of themselves enhance group inquiry as well as individual learning. And student responses to student questions are longer and more complex than their answers to teacher questions.

There are multiple ways of providing that students ask questions. But the alternative is only *that* they be provided for. Here we are not concerned with all the variety and detail of student questions as a topic in itself (see Chapter 2 for that), only insofar as it is an alternative to teacher questions.

There are only three cases to this alternative, and one and the same general way of enacting it in each case. Whether the case is the speaker's question, the class' question, or the discussion question, the alternative involves providing for a student question and then sustaining it for discussion.

Four generic steps or moves are involved (Fig. 5.2), two by the student and two by the teacher. The case begins, as all alternatives do, at the juncture where a student has just said something, as in answer to a question.

1. Student contribution.
2. Provide for a student question.
3. Student question.
4. Sustain student question.

There next begins a new sequence involving discussion of the student question. By contrast, the counterexample proceeds as follows:

1. Student contribution
2. Teacher question
3. Student answer
4. Teacher (a) evaluation of answer plus
           (b) further question

— at which point a new sequence not involving discussion has already begun.

The alternative is to provide for a student question. Generic examples will be given but no actual illustrations in this section. Students are rarely observed to ask questions in classrooms, whence

154

the uncommonly seen provisions made for them. Here the point is not the manner but the act of providing for student questions as an alternative to teacher questions. As a general caution, it should be noted that this act consists of more than mere words — actions and attitudes are required, along with appropriate conditions, purposes, and subject-matters (see Chapter 2). Therefore the *words* that are cited as examples in this section are merely instances of how in part to provide for student questions.

In short, you the teacher will have to work out the details appropriate to your purposes and circumstances. At issue here is the choice of student questions as one alternative to teacher questions during discussion. Instead of asking a question, this alternative provides for a student question — whether the speaker's question, the class' question, or the discussion question.

7. Speaker's question: Provide that the speaker formulate a question about what he has just said or is struggling to think and say

A student has just said 'Something is the case, I don't know' (Figure 5.2). You act so as to provide that he ask a question about that. For example, you say 'Relax for a minute and think up the question that's still bothering you about that.' In response the student poses a question, 'Is X the case?' You act to sustain the question for discussion. For example, you say 'You're wondering if X is the case. Good question.'

As a counterexample to the first teacher act, when the student has said that 'Something' is the case, you ask: 'What exactly do you think the case is?' He has just told you that he does not know what the case is, and you have just told him to tell you what the case is. 'Is it X? Is it Y? What do you think?' He thinks that some letter is the case but he doesn't know if it is X, if it is Y, if it is Z. 'Which letter is the case?' you helpfully ask. 'Roses have some color, I dunno' — 'Which color do roses have exactly?'

As a counterexample to the second teacher action, when the student does pose a question you either answer it or counter it.

(a) *Answer.* He says 'Is X the case?' and you say 'Yes' or 'No'. He has just told you that he is wondering whether X is the case and you have just told him that you do not wonder whether X is the case, you know that it is the case (or not). In that way you settle the issue, putting a stop to inquiry by helpfully substituting your certainty for his wonderment. 'I wonder if roses are red' — 'I know that roses are red, I don't wonder about it.' As much sense to say, 'No, violets are blue.'

155

(b) *Counter*. The other way not to do the alternative is to ask the student a question. When he asks 'Is X the case?' you wittily counter with 'Is X the case?' He has just told you that he is wondering whether X is the case, and you have just told him to wonder whether X is the case. Or you say 'Well, what do *you* think?' after he has told you what he is thinking. First he tells you that he can't tell, then you tell him to tell. In that way you handle the issue, stalling inquiry by helpfully supplying him with the question that he came up with in the first place, and by giving back to him the question that he has just contributed. 'Are roses red?' — 'What do *you* think? Are roses red?' As much sense to riposte 'Are violets blue?'

The alternative is to provide that the student ask a question and then to sustain it for discussion. In that way the student who is struggling to think and say something gets just the kind of help he needs to work his way out: help with identifying and formulating the question confusedly at issue in his mind. Once he gets his question, and only if he gets it, he can pursue the answer. Often enough you will hear the student begin working out the answer in the same breath as asking the question. Now the earlier struggle, confusion and difficulty with thinking and speaking begin to dissipate as energies mobilize and concentrate upon the newly-discovered issue that gives sense and direction to effort, by contrast to the earlier muddling and flailing about over scattered fragments of unseen but not unfelt issues.

The student's effort may still be difficult but now it is disciplined and promising, yielding one of two fruits. Either the student will work out the thought he was earlier, fruitlessly, struggling to express; or, if unable to answer his question, he will provide a new and perplexing question for everyone to consider. The action of the teacher helps the student to deliver himself of a stalled thought or to yield up a tough question as the fruit of his struggle to think. Either one is a good contribution to discussion. These are the goods that result from the teacher's enacted choice of this alternative.

8. Class question: Provide that another student pose a question about the speaker's contribution or the matter under discussion

A student has said that something is the case. You say, for example, 'Let's take a minute to hear the question that somebody else might be thinking about that.' The rest follows as before. In response some student says 'Is X the case?' and you sustain the question by saying, for example, 'You're wondering if X is the case. Good question'.

The counterexample is to ask the class for another statement of the case. One student has already made a statement, a confused and hesitant one: 'Something is the case, I don't know.' The teacher helpfully treats this contribution by ignoring it, turning to someone else for a clear and confident statement. 'Anybody else? What is the case here?' Whether the next student's statement is clear or not, the key issue is the treatment of the first contribution. What is to be done with it (as also with the next one)?

The choice is either to ask a question or to use an alternative. Any of the alternatives might be chosen at this juncture, but the kind being described here is provision for a student question. The previous case provided for the speaker's question; this case provides for the class' question. Instead of asking a question, then, the teacher treats the student's contribution ('Something is the case, I don't know') by providing that another student in the class pose a question related to it.

The choice seems odd — instead of a question from the teacher, a question from some student. But it is a well-grounded choice. First, of itself it enhances inquiry in the fact that *students* are formulating and posing questions. And it stimulates student thought and response, for the response consists of a question and questions stimulate the thought of those who ask them. But furthermore it encourages participation and enriches the exchange. That is because (1) students more readily address questions to students than to the teacher — a variant of the general case with social peers vs. subordinates; (2) students often ask better questions to each other than teachers do of them; (3) students respond to student questions at greater length and complexity than they do in answering teacher questions. Hence the teacher's act of providing for student questions has the overall effect of enhancing discussion on all counts.

9. Discussion question: Provide that students formulate the question that now appears at issue in the discussion

Some student has conclusively said that X is the case, and/or several have said that something is the case, X, Y, Z. At this juncture the teacher provides that the question for discussion be formulated by a student(s). You say, for example, 'Maybe it's time now to hear a few suggestions as to the kind of questions we should be asking now, given everything that has been said up to this point.' As before, some student says 'Is X the case?' and you sustain it by saying, for example, 'One question we might discuss now is whether X is the case. Interesting question.'

The counterexample is to state the next question for discussion. 'OK, so X is the case here. OK. Let's move on to the next question:

157

What is the case over there?' In that way you forestall inquiry by helpfully saving the students from wondering about what question comes next in the process. You also move discussion right along without making a big issue of what makes sense to be talked about at this point. You tell them what to talk about, and generally what to say: answers to your question. Otherwise, there's a lot of people in this room with different ideas that would take a lot of time to sort through and come together on, they're not that smart to begin with and they probably wouldn't agree anyway, even if somebody did come up with a good idea. Sensibly enough, you give them the next question to answer.

The alternative is discussion. You provide that students formulate the question that is now at issue. In that way you take steps to help them learn how to identify and formulate questions, how to connect question with question in a sequence of inquiry, how to join together in deliberating and deciding among competing and compelling issues, and how to act together under uncertainty. The result is a public question for discussion, one that arises from the group.

Suppose theirs is the wrong question? — to your way of thinking. Well, it would be nice if you had a way of thinking such that the question, 'Suppose it's a wrong question?' could never arise to worry you. If it does worry you, you can tell students that you think their question is the wrong one and you can offer your question as an alternative, whereupon you and they can discuss the qualifications of the two candidate questions. Or, even though it worries you, you can help them to proceed with a discussion based on the question they came up with and, should it eventually prove to be the wrong one, you can help them to discover and evaluate this turn of affairs and then return as before to take steps to help them learn to identify and formulate questions, etc. The result will again be a public question for discussion, one that arises from within the group. This is the question that *must* be discussed, so the discussants feel and experience. By contrast, the teacher's question need only be answered. And to do *that*, as the students know from long experience, requires no discussion.

Signals

Signal your reception of what the student is saying, without yourself taking or holding the floor. These are modest devices with substantial functions. There is nothing much to doing them, yet they encourage the speaker on and they open the floor for further participation. All the while they give a teacher something to say without actually holding the floor.

10. Phatics: Uttering a brief phrase, quietly exclaim feeling in reaction to what the speaker has just finished saying

He will then say more, and more than he will say in answer to a question.

When the student has said that X is the case (Figure 5.2), you exclaim, for example, 'Oh, X is so nice,' and he will go to say that Y is the case, too. 'Roses are red' — 'Oh, red roses are lovely!' — 'And violets are blue.' He has made a poem because of you. (Then you can exclaim that it is ugly.)

The phrasing of phatics will depend on the peculiarities of language around you. Perhaps people around you don't say things like 'lovely/nice'. You might say 'wonderful, amazing, interesting, awful'. Around me I used to hear 'Good gravy!' and 'Good night!' Other available phrases include: goodness, gracious, gosh, wow, no, well, my, you don't say!

Phatics are not reactions to the fact that the student has said something, nor evaluations of the way he has said it — as in, 'Good answer/lad'. You are not saying that the speaker, the move, or the wording of 'X is the case' is nice, you are saying that X is nice. Of course, if you don't feel that X is nice, don't exclaim so. And if you have no feeling at all about X, don't exclaim any feeling — that is, don't use a phatic but choose a more suitable alternative.

There is nothing to using phatics, and little enough has been said to describe them here. But you should know that, although modest in themselves, they serve important functions and have substantial effects on discussion. (As I learned from the experiments of D. and H. Wood, in the Correlated Readings.) Indeed, phatics are among the most powerful alternatives available. Responses to phatics are longer and richer than answers to questions of any type. X is indeed nice.

11. Fillers: Emitting some word or sound, indicate attentive interest in what the speaker has said or is saying

He will go on to say more. When the student says that X is the case, you emit, for example, 'Mm-humm'. He goes on to say that Y is the case. 'Roses are red' — 'Mm-humm' — 'and violets are blue.'

Fillers are more than modest, they are minimal. They are: 'mm-humm, uh-huh, mm, huhn, yes, yeah; I see/understand; good, fine, right, OK'. These are normal conversational devices, also called backchannel feedback, for signaling reception. They encourage the speaker by showing him that what he is saying is falling on not altogether deaf ears, and that the mind between them shall not for the moment venture forth to displace his own.

People respond positively to fillers, as in interviews; whether students respond to them more positively than to questions I do not know. Fillers remain a useful alternative if only for letting the teacher say at least something, *and* to say it without taking the turn at talk away from the student.

12. Pass: By gesture or statement, pass the next turn at talk to another speaker

The obvious response is more student talk, and talk by more students.

Student One says that X is the case. You pass by saying, for example, 'Yes, Student Two.' Student Two says that Y is the case. 'Roses are red' — Pass — 'Violets are blue.' Here two students join in to form a nice couplet by the teacher's gracious leave.

It is a fact of classroom life that students must have the teacher's leave to talk. The rule is that all turns at talk belong to the teacher. The teacher allocates turns to the students, while the next turn always belongs to him. Students expect the teacher to take it. Instead, he passes.

If you the teacher choose to pass, it is necessary that you do something to signal that choice. Students will not barge in, as peers will do with or without your leave. You might pass to a volunteer or supplicant by saying 'Yes' and/or by naming him; or by nodding, gesturing, smiling at him. You can pass to a non-volunteer or reticent by gazing contentedly and expectingly about the room, and/or by saying something like 'Some people haven't had a chance to speak yet.' But by all means do not make a pass at some reluctant student by saying something like a question. 'What do *you* think about it, John?' John and other wallflowers and fading violets will not be responsive; they will indeed answer, but certainly not with 'Violets are blue.'

By now you should know that the response will go as it did in the following child-care class. At the end of a rich discussion over how children feel when their parents divorce, and after several students have related their personal experiences and feelings at considerable length, the nice lady of the teacher gently but awkwardly passes to Karen and others who had not spoken.

T: How did *you* feel, Karen?
S: Oh, my parents got divorced when I was four or five.
T: How did they tell you?
S: I don't remember.

Next over to Kathy:

T: How about you, Kathy?
S: I don't remember.

Then over to Debbie:

T: Debbie, what about you?
S: No, not then.

Having come as far as to arrive at this twelfth alternative to questioning, you should by now know in general that questions are not the way to get Karen, Kathy, and Debbie to discuss; and you should know in particular eleven other ways to encourage their joining in. Specifically you should know how to make a pass at them. The alternative of 'Pass' by definition excludes asking a question and does not include much speech at all. But you must do something.

Pass is a minimal act but a substantial move on the teacher's part, ceding the turn and yielding the floor to student participation. It may seem to be a nothing, but the teacher is actually doing something to good purpose. In moments that you adjudge promising, your pass is a fundamental alternative with immediate beneficial effect on discussion.

Silences

Instead of asking a question, *say nothing at all*. Silences are either deliberate or non-deliberate. Only the deliberate kind are positive teacher behaviors, serving pedagogical purpose; the other kind reflect lack of pedagogy, serving to no good purpose. Non-deliberate silences are mentioned here to complete the list of possibilities and to show one way out of a bad situation. But the alternative of choice is to use deliberate silences.

161

13. Deliberate silence: Say nothing at all but maintain a deliberate, appreciative silence for three seconds or so

The original speaker will resume or another student will enter in.

Against all appearances, this is a positive teacher behavior; and seemingly against all expectations, students respond positively to it with both further talk and more complex thought.

For example (Figure 5.2), a student has just made some contribution, saying 'X is the case.' The teacher chooses not to ask a question and not to make a statement, nor to utter anything at all but to maintain an appreciative, attentive silence. After a few seconds the student says, 'And Y too is the case.' 'Roses are red,' — a noticeable pause, — 'and Violets are blue.' The speech is the student's, the intervening silence is the teacher's.

Everyone in the room notices that the teacher is doing something, not nothing. In a positive, active behavior he is deliberately maintaining silence, not a stony and withdrawn one but an appreciative, attentive one; and the silence itself is noticeable. To be noticeable the silence must achieve at least three seconds or so, for classroom exchanges are commonly rapid, following one upon the other with nary a pause. For the same reason, teachers are rarely observed to use silence and genuine examples of this alternative are hard to find.

Here a civics or government class is discussing capital punishment. A boy jumps in excitedly with a conclusion, phrased as a rhetorical question. The teacher remains silent and the boy resumes, now giving the antecedent reasoning.

S: So that's not consistent with the law, then, it is?
T: [three seconds]
S: — If rehabilitation is an object of sentencing and then they know that a [executed] killer is never going to be able to function again in society.

Or a different student may enter in after the silence to offer a divergent opinion, as in this discussion about life after death.

S1: I think it depends on what your definition of life after death is. And then I think, that each person has a different outlook on what it is like, what it'd be for them, for themselves.
T: [three seconds]
S2: It's already determined, the way that you live your life on earth . . . (continues for twelve seconds).

Or several students will contribute a range of complementary possibilities, as in this discussion of abortion:

S1: I guess it's just an easier way out.
T: [four seconds]
S2: Or maybe, their parents had high expectations of them, going to college . . . (continues for 21 seconds).

— and later:

S3: Yeah, parents are worried about, you know, 'What did I do wrong?' — teaching you to grow up, and all.
T: [four seconds]
S4: Or else they'll tell you that, 'If you marry so-and-so,' (continues for 13 seconds).

Deliberate silence is the simplest alternative available and one of the most effective. Yet it is also the hardest alternative to learn and to use. First of all, silence seems to be an awkward affair at best, if not a void, a waste of time or worse, counter-productive. Like other practitioners such as interviewers, teachers feel responsible for the flow of talk and the response of the client. They are concerned to keep entering in and saying something so that the student (or interviewee) will keep saying something back. Moreover, teachers feel responsible for moving through the curriculum and over the subject matter, keeping pace and covering ground. Lastly, teachers are responsible for managing the classroom, in some sense of discipline and crowd control. Silence threatens on each count. Actually to choose to use it seems not an alternative teaching behavior but an alternative to teaching.

The facts are otherwise. Deliberate silence can well serve pedagogical purpose in classroom discussions. The teacher remains in control, the subject is covered, and the students respond. Indeed, students respond with considerable length and complexity of thought. There are very good reasons that things turn out that way.

It is obvious that time is needed for thinking and for expression of thought. But more time is needed for more complex thought, and that is not so obvious. More time is needed both to develop *and* to express more complex thought.

If you ask someone to *describe* what is going on, say in a photograph, he will take a given amount of time to describe it to you. If you ask him to *explain* or *interpret* what is going on, he will take

163

a greater amount of time — not perforce saying more, only taking more time to say it. If the description contains ten words spoken in ten seconds, the explanation contains ten words spoken in twenty seconds — twice the time per word produced to express the more complex thought. Indeed, students in classroom discussions have been observed to take successively longer time — twice the time — to express successively 'higher' or more complex thought as they move from reciting things known to 'discussing' them: twice longer to state the facts than to recite a definition; twice longer again to proffer an explanation; and again twice longer to render a justification.

That is because the sustained expression of complex thought is marked by hesitations, false starts, and *pauses* in speech. It is at these precise points that teachers habitually enter to ask a question. But the student has only ostensibly finished speaking. Were the teacher to maintain silence at this juncture, he would likely hear not only further talk but also more complex thought. For example, this girl in a discussion on marriage is forming the possibility that her parents might not truly be married:

S: If they talked about their marriage. Like if they were just —
T: [five seconds]
S: — if they were talking about it, you know, like if they talked about marriage.
T: [three seconds]
S: And then all of a sudden I found out they weren't married. Then wouldn't they be lying to me all these years?

In another class a girl is pondering the difference between humans and animals:

S: Ah, I agree that we are the only ones who —
T: [four seconds]
S: — to a certain point, have the ability to distinguish between good and evil . . . (continues for 21 seconds).

Note how confused and unsatisfying these contributions are, and how appropriate it would seem for the teacher to say something helpful, perhaps asking a question for clarification. To the contrary, teacher silence at this juncture is appropriate pedagogy and furthermore it models appropriate discussion behavior for students to imitate. For instance, it models due attentiveness and appreciative listening until such time as a participant will have succeeded in delivering herself of her entire thought — not just a phrase or sentence or two. To speak up at the first second's pause or on the first flawed phrase is to grab the floor and to dismiss the speaker. It is no less an interruption than when someone is speaking. Indeed, someone *is* speaking — and thinking, too.

Such time is not usually given in classrooms, whether for developing or for expressing thought. Students are conditioned over the years to respond in staccato bursts of talk marked at every point by intervening teacher talk, especially questions. The observed lapse of time between the student's last syllable and the teacher's next word is less than a single second. City drivers will recognize this duration as just a touch longer than the lapse between the traffic light's changing to green and the honking of the taxi behind you. The alternative asks only that students be given three seconds' grace when they falter in giving expression to a complex thought that they are in process of forming about the issue before them in discussion.

Silence is a very odd teacher behavior to which everyone in the room will have to accustom themselves, and which you the teacher will just have to learn in the first place. Let us presume that the major obstacle to your learning it is now cleared away — the complex of pressing concerns and suspicious attitudes about the utility of silence. Naturally you still have this complex but we will pretend that you don't, so that we can pass on to the remaining difficulties. They are all minor ones.

The first thing you have to learn is just how long three seconds lasts, the empirical duration. You can learn this at home, as I did, with the second's hand on a clock or stopwatch, or a metronome. The second thing to learn is timing. You can practise timing as you recite something — separate sentences — before a mirror or other friendly face who might provide helpful cues. The third thing to learn is how to do it in your classroom, in the heat of the exchange.

There in the classroom, where everyone is accustomed to rapid exchanges and when students expect you to speak up within less than a second's lapse, three seconds of silence will seem an eternity, especially when manifold concerns press upon you while you are standing up there in front and nothing seems to be happening. So *despite* good intentions and earnest practice, you rush things and start talking to get something going. That is the hard way to do things, as I did them. Now there is an easier way that I have thought of for you, which I myself have tested for you in several forbidding

165

circumstances. It is foolproof. All you have to do is sing 'Baa, baa, black sheep.'

A student says, 'X is the case' (Fig. 5.2). You stand there singing in your mind:

Baa, baa, black sheep
Have you any wool?

On the 'baa, baa' you nod, nod to the student, hoping he has more wool. That takes up a good four seconds which you will run in two or three. At that point, unbelievably enough, the student says, 'And Y too, come to think about it.'

Then you decide what to do next with this response — which other alternative to use, or which question to pose. You might even choose again to use deliberate silence, pursuing what you judge to be a particularly rich development in the discussion. If that is the case, sing the rest of 'Baa, baa, black sheep.'

The full pursuit, should you judge it promising at the moment, starts as before with a student who says that X is the case (see Figure 5.2). You do your 'Baa, baa' and he adds that Y is the case, too. Again you maintain a deliberate silence for three seconds or so, singing along in your mind:

Yes sir, yes sir
Three bags full

— with a nod, nod, hold for three seconds!

If you hold out for three bags full, that student or another will say, 'But not Z — Z isn't the case.' So you sing:

One for my master
One for my dame,
One for the little boy
Who lives in the lane.

— looking gently at the speaker, next at some girl, then at some boy, finally glancing down the back row. You are going the full course of silence at this rich juncture, fully eight or nine seconds which you do in five, whereupon a student starts explaining that 'Z is not the case here, because . . .'

All this may sound silly enough but it is serious business to enhance the students' cognitive, affective, and expressive processes, facilitating discussion and perhaps even learning. And it is hard to do. 'Baa, baa, black sheep' is merely an artifice for enacting the choice of an alternative teacher behavior, deliberate silence, in service of educational purpose in this classroom circumstance. That is good pedagogy.

14. Non-deliberate silence: When silence occurs that is not deliberate, you better figure out something to do

Non-deliberate silence is not of your choosing and acting, and describes a situation where no known and good purpose is being served. Confusion and trouble surfaces or events and people are suspended while you are silent for want of speech and action.

Figure out something to do. For example, in the case where things are troubled and you sense you are losing control, start asking questions. A student has said, 'X is the case.' Confusion and trouble arises and you start to lose your grip. Put a question to some student and he will answer. Put another question for another answer, and yet a further question and answer, and so on. Chances are that you will regain control of the class' social and verbal behavior. But you have already lost the discussion and it will not return for the duration. The class is now in a recitation mode at best. You can make another try at discussion tomorrow.

For the moment you have chosen and enacted the best alternative available to your judgement in service of your purposes in present circumstances. Later you will reflect on your enacted choice, assessing and re-planning. That is good pedagogy. Perhaps tomorrow discussion will proceed thanks to it and you.

USING QUESTIONS AND ALTERNATIVES

During a discussion the use of the above alternatives — deliberate silence, signals, student questions, various statements — promises to serve pedagogical purposes in ways that teacher questions are widely expected to do but commonly cannot. In service of these purposes the teacher enacts a choice of alternatives.

Service to purpose

Three broad purposes that teachers have for their action concern learning the subject-matter, facilitating the classroom process, and learning how to learn.

167

Learning to discuss

The use of alternatives teaches students appropriate discussion behaviors, serving the one broad purpose of learning how to learn. The teacher's action models for students a given behavior appropriate at some juncture; it evokes a complementary behavior in response; and it precludes inappropriate behaviors. These three aspects of the action serve both the immediate exchange and subsequent exchanges.

For example, by making a reflective restatement you are showing students how and when that behaviour is to be performed. In subsequent exchanges students might imitate that model, by themselves offering a reflective restatement before going on to act otherwise on their presumed understanding of what the speaker has said.

In the meantime, your behavior evokes a complementary behavior in reaction. For example, the speaker responds by confirming or qualifying your restated understanding, adding clarification or elaboration as needed for student and teacher to achieve a shared understanding. Now, for future exchanges, students will know better how to act in response to the selected alternative. They already know what to do when the teacher asks a question; they have to *learn* how to act in response to the strange alternative behavior.

Finally, the enactment of the alternative precludes inappropriate related behaviors. A reflective restatement, for example, of itself displaces inappropriate behaviors that arise to claim a place in the discussion at that juncture. The complementary behaviour that it evokes in response occupies the next place, again pre-empting inappropriate claims. By enacting the alternative, you fill the room with two positive discussion behaviors *and* you forestall two possible negative ones. For instance, the alternative substitutes for impulsive expression of self's opinion a reflective statement of the other's meaning and, in response, evokes a fruitful clarification in place of a pointless argument. In addition to precluding these at the immediate juncture, the alternative helps students gradually to diminish inappropriate behaviors in subsequent exchanges.

In sum, the use of alternatives serves the broad purpose of learning how to learn, by teaching the students appropriate discussion behaviors that serve both in the immediate exchange and in subsequent exchanges. An appropriate behavior A is performed and modelled at a given juncture; students might later imitate A at a similar juncture. A complementary behavior A' is evoked in response to A; students now know how to respond to later instances of A. Inappropriate behaviors Anti-A and Anti-A' are precluded at this juncture; students reduce the frequency of their Anti-A and Anti-A' behaviors. The teacher is helping students learn to discuss, by the very act of implicating them in the alternative behaviors. All the while the teacher is also fostering discussion.

Fostering discussion

A second broad purpose of teacher action is to facilitate the class-room process at hand, so that it goes well and smoothly and perhaps eventuates in learning. The use of alternatives fosters discussion by enhancing the students' cognitive, affective and expressive processes.

These general effects were illustrated by numerous individual examples for the various alternatives presented. Extensive illustrations are found in the Appendix, showing how selected alternatives function in discussions of three different kinds conducted by Mr S, Mr P, and Mr W. As a useful exercise, you may examine these cases and compare the effects of the alternatives and questions used by these teachers. Overall the contrast may be summarized as follows.

There is greater participation. There is more student talk: more students talk; and students talk more, both overall and at each turn at talk. There is more student-student talk: students talk more with each other; and students refer more to other students' contributions.

There is deeper personal involvement. Students proffer more contributions and more elaborate ones; they contribute more outside topics and material, more personal experiences, feelings, attitudes and meanings; they initiate more and sustain initiative in a more active, independent dynamic.

There is more complex thought. Students evaluate and justify, opine and explain, clarify and counter, interpret and apply, analyze and synthesize. These are often called the 'higher-cognitive' processes.

There is richer inquiry. Students explore and speculate more, pondering and wondering. Students say things in a more questioning way, and students ask more questions.

By providing for richer inquiry, more complex thought, deeper personal involvement, and greater participation, the alternatives enhance the students' cognitive, affective, and expressive process. That is to foster discussion.

Learning subject-matter

A third broad purpose of teacher action is that students learn that which is being taught. The alternatives give promise of learning only inasmuch as they are conducive to discussion and only insofar as discussion is conducive to that which is to be taught and learned. Alternatives may be the right choice for discussion, while discussion might be the wrong choice for learning. Does the use of these alternatives enhance student *learning*? No one knows. It is a good question.

Choice of action

Questions and alternatives display choices for action. In general, during a discussion the recommended choice is to use some alternative. No specific one is to be preferred but a mix is useful, each chosen as you judge suitable at a given juncture. It is silly to act as if you were always supposed to use this or that alternative. Moreover, there is a time when the preferred choice is no alternative but to ask a question.

The time to ask a question is when you are personally perplexed to know. By all means ask that question. When not perplexed, by all means use an alternative. Your occasional perplexed question, arising by contrast to a dozen alternatives and in complement to the perplexed questions from students, enacts the most promising of all choices for teaching and learning during discussion.

Reflection on enacted choice

What will be the educative fruits, in your classroom, of using a mix of alternatives together with an occasional perplexed question? Only you can tell. Try it and see.

Some research has been done on this issue. It may offer an answer, but your answer can be found only in your practice of enacted choices in service of your purposes in your classroom circumstances.

Much argument and exhortation has been proposed in this chapter. It may convince and persuade you to action, but it does not answer the questions. The answer is found in the consequences of your enacted choices.

Some teachers may have experience with using these alternatives and with using questions. That may answer the question for them, but your answer can be found only in your reflected experience. Our shared experience can be helpful when we reflect on it together, yet that serves mainly to inspire us to renew our efforts, encouraging one another to action.

170

These are the alternatives that someone else has discovered and knows in theory, in research, and in practice. You will find other alternatives. You will come to know them in theory by artfully conceiving the world of questioning and teaching. You will know them in research by systematically observing their use in your teaching and their effects on learning. You will know them in practice by choosing to enact them in your classroom, by reflecting on the enacted choices and their consequences, and by making new designs on action to serve pedagogical purpose in your classroom circumstance.

Please try it and see for yourself. Then you will learn the use of questions and alternatives during discussion, and your students will learn to question and to discuss.

CORRELATED READINGS

A Education

Boggs, S.T. (1972) 'The meaning of questions and narratives to Hawaiian children', in C.B. Cazden, V.P. John and D. Hymes (eds.), *Functions of language in the classroom*, New York: Teachers College — field study comparing questions and 'other verbalizations'.

Dillon, J.T. (1979) 'Alternatives to questioning', *High School Journal, 62*, 217–222; Dillon, J.T. (1981) 'To question and not to question during discussion: II. Nonquestioning techniques', *Journal of Teacher Education, 32* (6) 15–20 — description and rationale for six or seven 'alternatives' to questioning.

Dillon, J.T. (1981) 'To question and not to question during discussion: I. Questioning and discussion', *Journal of Teacher Education, 32* (5), 51–55 — an easy essay on the place of questions in discussion.

Dillon, J.T. (1981) 'Duration of response to teacher questions and statements', *Contemporary Educational Psychology, 6*, 1–11; Dillon, J.T. (1982) 'Cognitive correspondence between question/statement and response', *American Educational Research Journal, 19*, 540–551; Dillon, J.T. (1985) 'Using questions to foil discussion', *Teaching and Teacher Education, 1*, 109–121 — correlational and case studies comparing questions and statements (and other alternatives in 1985 study).

Dillon, J.T. (1981) 'Discussion characteristics in a sample of religion and social studies classes', *Character Potential: A Record of Research, 9*, 203–205 — a descriptive study of a dozen characteristics observed in high school discussion classes.

Dillon, J.T. (1983) 'Cognitive complexity and duration of classroom speech', *Instructional Science, 12*, 59–66 — a study of the increasingly longer time it takes students to say increasingly more complex things (e.g., definitions, explanations).

Dillon, J.T. (1984) 'Research on questioning and discussion', *Educational Leadership*, *42* (3), 50–56 — an easy review, for teachers, of theoretical, empirical, and pedagogical literature on questioning and discussion.

Dillon, J.T. (ed.) (1987) *Questioning and discussion: A multidisciplinary study*, Norwood, N.J.: Ablex — a collection of twelve analyses by scholars from different perspectives, all bearing on one set of actual classroom discussions — including the very transcripts reproduced in the Appendix to this present book.

Tobin, K. (1987) 'The role of wait time in higher cognitive level learning', *Review of Educational Research*, *57*, 69–95 — review of studies on 'wait-time', or silent pauses before and after questions.

Wood, H. and Wood, D. (1983) 'Questioning the preschool child', *Educational Review*, *35*, 149–162; Wood, H. and Wood, D. (1984) 'An experimental evaluation of the effects of five styles of teacher conversation on the language of hearing-impaired children', *Journal of Child Psychology and Psychiatry*, *25*, 45–62 — experimental studies comparing questions and 'phatics' and 'comments'.

Other fields

Colby, K.M. (1961) 'On the greater amplifying power of causal-correlative over interrogative inputs on free association in an experimental psychoanalytic situation', *Journal of Nervous and Mental Disease*, *133*, 233–239 — experimental study comparing questions and 'causal-correlative' statements.

Frank, G.H. and Sweetland, A. (1962) 'A study of the process of psychotherapy: The verbal interaction', *Journal of Consulting Psychology*, *26*, 135–138 — study comparing questions and 'clarification of feeling' and 'interpretation'.

Hubbell, R.D. (1977) 'On facilitating spontaneous talking in young children', *Journal of Speech and Hearing Disorders*, *62*, 216–231 — sophisticated discussion on how to 'facilitate' talking without 'eliciting' it by questions.

McComb, K.B. and Jablin, F.M. (1984) 'Verbal correlates of interviewer emphathic listening and employment interview outcomes', *Communication Monographs*, *51*, 353–371 — study comparing questions and 'restatements', 'verbal encouragers', and 'latencies' or silent pauses.

Prutting, C.A. et al. (1978) 'Clinician-child discourse: Some preliminary questions', *Journal of Speech and Hearing Disorders*, *63*, 123–139 — study of questions and various statements.

Rochester, S.R. (1973) 'The significance of pauses in spontaneous speech', *Journal of Psycholinguistic Research*, *2*, 51–81 — review of studies from various fields.

Snow, D.A., Zurcher, L.A., and Sjoberg, G. (1982) 'Interviewing by comment: An adjunct to the direct question', *Qualitative Sociology*, *5*, 385–411 — description and rationale for eight types of 'comment' in lieu of questions.

PRACTICAL EXERCISES

1. Conduct a discussion on this chapter

With the concurrence of your course instructor, select five or so agreeable fellow students in this course for a half-hour of discussion directed by you as teacher. Perhaps you and another student can each conduct a discussion with different groups of fellow students, while the rest of the class observes and later offers helpful comments, followed by a whole-class discussion on your discussion about questioning and discussion. If you are not a student, perhaps you can discuss this chapter with an agreeable colleague who will first read it with you.

2. Formulate the question for discussion

You and other-students in this course can each formulate 'the question for discussion' that you would pose if conducting a discussion on this chapter — and/or on any other readings and topics in this course. Together you then discuss the alternative candidates for the discussion question. As one point for discussion, you might anticipate the possible answers and evaluate the state that a class would be in once having discussed the question.

3. Formulate the question that this chapter answers

Then formulate the answer that it gives, making a single question-answer proposition. Next evaluate the chapter by questioning its validity and usefulness as an answer to that question. Several students might each formulate the question-answer of this chapter and join in a discussion over their alternative formulations.

4. Analyze the questions and alternatives used in the discussions in the Appendix

There you will find three discussions of different kinds conducted by Mr P, Mr S, and Mr W. Identify the questions and alternatives used, and assess and compare their effects on that discussion. Then compare your analysis against this chapter and/or against Dillon's analysis of these same three discussions as published in *Teaching and Teacher Education*, 1985; or to any of the twelve other analyses by various scholars in the anthology, *Questioning and Discussion* (see Correlated Readings pp. 171 and 172). Students might team up to analyze one or another of the discussions, then the various teams can report and discuss their analyses and comparisons.

5. Do a critical inspection of this chapter's presentation of alternatives to questioning

For each alternative, look for completeness of presentation if you can find it: name and description; illustration by generic and specific examples; contrast with questioning; rationale for using the alternative; and suggestions for learning how to use it. Evaluate selected points of interest — the aptness of illustration, the persuasiveness of rationale, etc. Compare the entire section against the generic scheme of pedagogy proposed in previous chapters and, or course, against notions that you and others have about teaching and learning, and about questioning and discussion.

6. Try using a selected alternative during a discussion in some course you are attending

Do this exercise as a *student*, not as a teacher but as a participant in the discussion. If not in a course, try it during a conversation among friends or colleagues.

7. Converse with a child without asking a single question

The next time that you are introduced to a child or meet up with one in some social situation, start speaking to him with some statement and continue otherwise to avoid questions for at least your next five turns at talk. Ponder the result on the *child's* talk. Wonder about using alternatives with the children sitting before you in your classroom.

174

8. Try speaking in questions during some conversation with peers

The next time that you find yourself in some social situation, pick a point in the conversation and ask a question, then ask another question at your every turn at talk. See how long your friends or fellow teachers will let you get away with that. Note the particular device they use to stop you. Wonder about asking questions during your classroom discussions.

9. Arrange that you experience being asked questions about something that you do not understand

You will need a naive confederate, someone not in this course. You will also need something (an issue, a book, an event, etc.) that can be understood in various ways and that you do not have any clear understanding of. The confederate does have a clear understanding or position. You do not tell him to ask you questions; you let the confederate help you to understand by discussing the matter with you in his own way. Note the effect on you of the questions asked of you, and compare that to the questions that you ask. Wonder about the usefulness to students' understanding, of their questions and yours during a discussion in your classroom.

10. Practise listening and responding to students

You will need to tape-record any one of your classes during which you plan to make a deliberate effort to listen to what students say. That night, recall all of the student responses that you can, writing them down or speaking them into a tape-recorder. Then compare your recall with the record of the class.

Pursue this exercise by replaying selected student contributions and then, stopping the tape, voice aloud a 'reflective restatement'. Vary the exercise by voicing other selected alternatives after this same student contribution, replaying it each time. Then let the tape go to hear what you actually did say at that juncture. Reflect on your enacted choice and its consequences, and design a suitable choice for action in tomorrow's discussion.

And since you already have the tape-recording, do Exercise 4 with it.

Appendix

Classroom Transcripts

MR H's RECITATION — American Revolution

1a. What — I want to go into another question about his military capabilities. What was it that made him militarily successful? What was it about his strategy that enabled him to be successful? (Howard) [teacher — 11 seconds]

b. He didn't fight straight out like the British. He fought behind brick walls, trees, and stuff like that. (b—6) [boy — 6 seconds]

2a. Did you read anywhere in the book where his army was destroyed? (t—6)

b. No. (s—1)

3a. That his army was destroyed — did you see that anywhere? That Washington's army was destroyed? (t—6)

b. Not completely. (s—1)

4a. Not completely? (Tony) (t—1)

b. They were outsmarted, but not destroyed. (b—3)

5a. Well, is there a difference between those two statements? (t—3)

b. Yeah, there is. (b—1)

6a. Well, what is that difference? (t—1)

b. To be outsmarted — out of the larger army. (b—4)

c. Other than that, if you're destroyed, you're destroyed, you're dead. (b—2)

7a. If they're destroyed, they're dead? And what if they are outsmarted? (t—5)

b. That means they could get by or move into better territory. (b—5)

8a. So, what do you think Washington's success was as a military leader? — taking into context, you know, tactics and so on. (Tony) (t—9)

b. He was always taking it step by step, he never wanted to be outsmarted. (b—4)

9a. But you said he was, at times. (t—2)

b. Right, yeah, but then you asked what about his success. (b—3)

10a. Well, why is it that he — (ah, Jim) (t—2)

b. He was able to go back and fight harder; even after he was outsmarted, he was able to get 'em back on the rebound. (b—7)

11a. Ah, because why? (Chris) (t—2)

b Maybe he had to learn by the mistakes that happened, to learn by them and realize what it was that had gone wrong. (g—11)

12a. Well, did the colonies have a large army? (t—2)

b. No, they — I don't know. (g—4)

13a. Those of you who worked on that question about the army, and some of the problems of wartime government — what did you find out about the army itself? (Howard) (t—8)

b. Well, the colonial army was really outnumbered by the British. Some of the people — the lack of interest by some of the colonies and stuff like that — most of the colonies had to fight it by themselves, so they were outnumbered. (b—16)

14a. Well, OK, how did one get to be a member of the army? By way of the draft? (t—5)

b. No, more or less by volunteering. (b—2)

15a. By volunteering. Could Congress, could Congress tell the states to furnish more men? (t—9)

b. No, I don't think so. (b—1)

16a. What did Congress have to do? (t—2)

b SILENCE (4 seconds) (x—4)

17a. Now, you're on the right track. What did Congress have to do in order to get more men into the army? (t—4)

b. I guess make it worth their while. (b—2)

18a. Well, let's get away from pay. Let's assume that wages are not a factor at the moment. If the army is a volunteer army, as such, where did people volunteer to? (t—11)

b. SILENCE (5 seconds) (x—5)

19a. In other words, were there national offices established by Congress to which a person went that wanted to volunteer? (t—10)

b. You'd just go find where the army was, and join it. (b—2)

20a. Not exactly. They went by way of what vehicle, do you know? (t—6)

b. — their colonies back home. (g—6)

21a. That's right, they went by way of each colony. So, what we're saying, then, is that Congress could not merely order a colony to furnish more men. It had to ask a colony for more men. And if people did not volunteer into that colonial army — the Virginia army, for instance, the South Carolina army — if people didn't then they just didn't. So, Washington commanded an all-volunteer army. And another problem with that army — in addition to just sheer numbers, it's not professional as such, it's all volunteer, and people come and go as they want to. Now, when you have a person leading that type of a military group, you certainly are not leading a professional army, and something that he does with it is very important. It's not that large — probably the most they ever had at one time was maybe 5,000 people. He never permits what little army they had to be destroyed. But that's not to say he never lost. (t—59)

MS HT's RECITATION — Mayflower Compact

1a. All right, OK. Let's go back to the Mayflower Compact. — Now wait a minute, don't turn to your book. Let's just think something out here. What did those people agree to before they got off the boat? Now that was, you know, about 100 of them that were on the boat, more or less. There were more actually. And women of course had no say-so, no say-so whatever. But what did those men on that boat agree to, before they got off the boat? (Nina) [teacher — 36 seconds]

b. Self-government. (g—2)

c. SILENCE (4 seconds)

2a. Yes, but I wish you'd explain it to me. You know, you're giving me a phrase that I've used over and over, and it's a phrase used in your book; but when you don't put it into a — into the context of a discussion, I don't really know what you're saying. I just want to know very simply — Here you have 100 people, who didn't have much more than the clothes on their back; who were about 3,000 miles from what was their home; on foreign shores, and they didn't know anything what was ahead of them. The shelter they were going to have for the next couple of weeks wasn't even there; they were going to have to make their own shelter. The food that they had was probably pretty well run out. Now, what did these people agree to, on that boat, the Mayflower? (Darryl?) (t—54)

b. [unintelligible] (boy — 3 seconds)

3a. Who was going to make the rules? (t—1)

b. [response] (4 seconds)

4a. All right, did they have any restrictions on themselves? (t—3)

b. Yes. (b—1)

5a. What? (t—1)

b. [response] (2 seconds)

6a. OK, did they have to own property? (t—2)

b. No. (b—1)

7a. Why did they decide among themselves, 'We will go by what the majority here wants?' Why did they make it that simple? 'And when we get off this boat and we settle on that land, we're going to make our own rules.' Did they put any restrictions on themselves on that boat — any limitations? (Lydia) (t—21)

b. No. (g—1)

8a. Why do you suppose they didn't (t—2)

b. [response] (4 seconds)

9a. And were they all interested? (t—2)

b. Mm-mm. (g—1)

10a. Sure, they were interested. They were all very much concerned. Well then, why do you suppose 150 years later, or 100 years later, they come up with the idea, 'Oh, we gotta have property qualifications in order for you to have the right to vote' —? Why do you suppose that restriction came into existence? (Lydia) (t—28)

b. [response] (11 seconds)

11a. All right, I'm sure they did. And also, as time went on, within 100 years, you had people who accumulated wealth, and people who in time accumulate wealth, and accumulate things, they have a very vital interest. And so they also have a tendency frequently to become very influential too, don't they? Listen, name me an influential person in Chicago — anybody. (Sylvia) (t—28)

b. Mayor Bilandic. (g--1)

12a. All right, Mayor Bilandic. He's a millionaire, isn't he? (t—6)

b. [murmurs] (3 seconds)

13a. Well, I read that he's a millionaire. What was he before he was elected to the City Council? What did he do for a job, for an occupation? Anybody know? (Darryl) (t—11)

b. [response] (3 seconds)

14a. Well now, before he got into politics, what did he do for a living? (t—4)

b. He was a lawyer. (b—1)

15a. He was a lawyer, right. He had a good law practice. Name me another influential person, in Chicago. (Darryl) (t—10)

b. Gov. Thompson. (b—1)

16a. He's not in Chicago. I want it to be restricted to Chicago. He lived around here at one time. I don't know if he lived in Chicago or Evanston. And he was a law professor, taught law at Northwestern University. Give me a name of another influential person. Oh, come on, where are your imaginations, you people!? Anybody. You know, about three-fourths of you haven't spoken yet? Give me any inlfuential citizen in this city. (Darryl) (t—36)

b. Cecil Partee. (b—1)

17a. Cecil Partee. Look at that, Darryl — she wants to know who he is. Is he from Chicago? (t—9)

b. Yeah. (b—1)

18a. All right, I don't know; he is a prominent member of the Illinois Assembly. He's a black leader. All right, give me some others — but give me in Chicago; you know, Cecil Partee does all of his work down in Springfield. (All right, Sylvia) (t—16)

b. Jackson . . . (g—5)

19a. Jesse Jackson. All right, he certainly is. Do you think he's wealthy? (t—6)

b. [murmurs] (2 seconds)

20a. Yeah, I see him driving around in a — I shouldn't say I see — I hear he drives around in a Cadillac. Is that right? (t—6)

b. [response] (4 seconds)

21a. Al right, he's working for a cause that he believes in. He certainly has access to a lot of money, doesn't he? (t—7)

b. [response] (2 seconds)

22a. All right. And he is influential. I don't know how wealthy he is. You hear different things. All right, give me somebody else. Anybody. Come on, shoot off here!

MR L's RECITATION — French–Indian War [Seven Years' War]

1a. Yeah, then England would lose the area over here. So, it was
. . . So, the Albany plan didn't really particularly work. Ah,
what — why did the English eventually win the war? Why did
the English eventually win the war? [teacher — 56 seconds]

b. The French were outnumbered. (b—5)

2a. The French were badly outnumbered, 20 to 1. See, the
French people didn't really come over here to settle, they just
came over to make money, on what two items? (As we're
going to hear from Morina on Monday.) (t—14)

b. Fur and fish. (ss—2)

3a. Fish and fur. Fish and furs. That's what they were interested
in. The English, a lot of the English people came over here,
not because they wanted to make a lot of money and then go
back to England; they just wanted to be here, period. Why?
Didn't like it over there. What reason? (Tom) Why didn't
they like it over there? (t—19)

b. [response] (1 second)

4a. What was one of the big reasons? (t—1)

b. I don't know. (b—1)

c. Religious difficulties. (b—1)

5a. Religious difficulties, right? They weren't allowed to worship
the way they wanted to . . . Now I would like to make sure
you realize how these particular wars were fought.
Remember — why did — you know, what are the, some of
the particular or peculiar circumstances in a war at that
particular time in history? Why did Braddock lose, at
Duquesne, when he tried to capture DuQuesne? (Tom)
(t—38)

b. Because he was wearing red clothes, and they spotted them.
(b—3)

6a. They spotted them. Not only that, but they did what? (t—3)

b. They marched in formation. (Hold it, Sam. What?) (b—3)

7a. They marched in a certain predictable formation. (t—3)

b. [unintelligible] (5 seconds)

8a. And how would you do that? And how would you fight the
Indians? Or, how did the Indians fight? (t—4)

b. (—sneaked—) (b—2)

9a. Sneaked around, behind trees and rocks, and so on. . . . You
fought according to rules, and you didn't fight, for instance,
during planting time or harvest time. You only fought when

you didn't have anything else to do. Or anything worthwhile. That's a little over-drawn. (t—36)

b. [unintelligible] (3 seconds)

10a. Probably not at night, either. It was . . . Now, what were the two biggest forts that would be coveted by the French and the English? One was — (t—75)

b. DuQuesne. (b—1)

11a. DuQuesne, all right. Where is it again? (t—3)

b. Pittsburgh. (b—1)

12a. Pittsburgh, right at the triangle. . . . Why couldn't you go overland? (t—16)

b. Take too long. (b—1)

13a. Why did it take too long? (t—1)

b. Mountains. (b—1)

14a. Well, mountains. But what's the biggest thing, in a way? (t—2)

b. Forest. (b—1)

15a. Forest, it was solid forest. Now, . . .

MR P's DISCUSSION — multiple personality

1a. So, Eve White the quiet introvert, was the most dominant. OK, now we're back to the question. We're trying to solve, with the little bit of psychology that we have — we know it's dysfunctional to have three personalities — we want to help this woman to have one personality. How — what might we do? (Gabriella) [teacher — 21 seconds]

b. I think that you could try to, ah, get Eve White to see herself as Eve Black, and ah, once she sees herself like this, then, whatever's causing this, split personality, she might try and deal with both of them, and make both one personality, and change it. Because, I wouldn't knock them out, I would combine them. (g—28)

2a. Do you think there'd be an advantage of knocking them out? (t—3)

b. Yeah, if you knocked both out. (g—4)

3a. If you knocked Eve White and Eve Black out, and left Jane? (t—4)

b. Well, aren't Eve White and Eve Black Jane? (b—3)

c. [unintelligible] (3 seconds)

4a. What would be the danger of that? Why not, as one solution, why not destroy the first two — if you had the psychological tools — and leave Jane? (t—11)

b. That's what we want to do. (g—5)

5a. That's what you want to do? (t—1)

b. That's why I'd combine them, you know — Eve Black and Eve White. But you can't do that. (g—6)

6a. Well, supposing you have the tools? In other words, supposing you have the psychological know-how to knock out two personalities. Now, from what you know, is that a good idea? (t—9)

b. Yeah, I think so/I don't think so. (Duane) (s—3)

c. Wouldn't she gain another personality? (Say that again) Wouldn't she gain another personality? (b—9)

7a. How do you know — that's a good question — how do you know she wouldn't gain another personality? You got rid of Black and White; you got Jane left; how do you know she wouldn't get another one? (t—11)

b. [unintelligible] (3 seconds) (Mitchell)

c. I said, how do you know that the two that you knocked out, and the one that you left, are suitable? — the one that's left is — the original one? (b—9)

8a. I don't know. (Yvonne) (t—3)

b. OK, now, first I would — if I was the psychiatrist, I would go all the way back to her childhood. And I'd find out from her how she was — not from her but, you know, through other sources — ask them exactly how she was as a child, even when she was one or two years old, because it did say that, in the book, that her split personality started as far back as a child. I mean, as far back as when she was a child, she used to do, you know — get into different things. Then I would — I wouldn't knock out — (g—42)

9a. Stop there for a moment, Yvonne. Supposing you take this approach — what do you expect to find? If you have a grown woman winding up in your office with three personalities — what do you expect to find back there in her childhood? (t—16)

b. Something that could have flared up or something. (g—4)

10a. Like what. (t—1)

b. I don't know! That's what we're looking for! (g—3)

11a. OK, come on, let's find it! (Mike) (t—2)

b. You'd probably expect to find problems she had at home, you know — like mistreatment from her parents. (b—7)

12a. How would that — (t—1)

b. 'Cause, ah, like it set up, like, insecurity — and she might look for something else inside herself to compensate for that, so she developed a new personality. (OK. Darryl) (b—12)

c. OK, like getting back to the childhood thing — like see who her idols were. See where the person had her idols. (b—12)

13a. OK, but how would that — if you found out who her heroes or her idols were, what would that have to do with splitting off into two personalities? (Terrence) (t—9)

b. Wouldn't you want to try and be like your idol? You know, if you were idolized, you know, you were more or less one of the big idols, to a certain point. Then like, ah, she had an auntie that was shot, and you know, she admired her for the way she was — maybe she'd be shot down as long as she's like her auntie. She'll go home and see that her mother is a nice housewife. She'd want to be like that. Or somebody else — her friends — something like that. (b—35)

14a. We all experience what you just said! How come — so it — don't we? (Yeah.) How come she wound up in such a, such a dump? (t—11)

b. Well, wouldn't that be some kind of restrictions in her background that wouldn't allow her to do that, such as her parents not letting her do something, to the point that she had to, like, ah — (g—14)

15a. Did you see the movie? (t—1)

b. No. (g—1)

16a. No. OK, something like that is suggested in the movie — that the trauma was so great that it caused the creation of a new personality. (Duane) (t—10)

b. It could be like — you want to do something like that, . . . go with the stronger personality . . . a person, you know, like is reading a lot of books and stuff like that . . . 'I want to be just like her'. (b—26)

17a. OK, I think you'd have to put that together with trauma. That kind of idea, that several of you have expressed, put that together with trauma. In other words, if you try to imitate as a little child, your idols, and you were severely punished for it — this is just one general example — then, for whatever reasons, you might be forced to split in two. I think that's the only way I can put it together — it's been a long time since I read that. (Yvonne) (t—33)

b. OK, Isn't it true that whatever your conscious mind turns out,

184

your subconscious reacts, don't it, right? Now, say she's saying to herself — she's getting it in her mind that she wants to be just like that lady, and her subconscious mind's gonna pick up on that and react on that, and she's gonna start acting like a certain person, doing the same kind of things that certain person do, you know — she's gonna pick up that personality, act that person. (g—37)

18a. You're working — we're working on one model now, aren't we? We're working on the idol model. I wonder if there are others. (Mike) (t—10)

b. There's got to be others, 'cause you can have a personality that you develop under, you know, constant conflict. Like a child might be exposed to two opposites and it's always rehearsing, it's always going on, over and over and over again. OK? The child might be split into each one of those worlds, in order to deal with it. (b—22)

19a. OK, good. That wasn't in the book either. If there's so much conflict — if there's so much conflict, you might have to shift gears without even knowing it, just to protect the self — is the model that he's using, the conflict model. (Anthony) (t—15)

b. What about like, an overprotective parent and stuff? Like, you can be very shy and things like that. And maybe she had parents that told her, you know, that she shouldn't go out with no guys, or nothing like that . . . that wasn't the kind of person she was. She was a little more outgoing. And maybe when she was young and that, maybe that . . . her parents had a real overpowering effect on her. That could change her. (b—31)

20a. OK, how many of you read *I never promised you a rose garden*? — Hannah Green's book.

MR S' DISCUSSION — sex in family life

1a. Someone else want to address themselves? What were the patterns of behavior in your family in regards to these three things? (Tony) [teacher — 6 seconds]

b. In my house, they were very strict on the kids, they didn't wanna talk about sex or nothing like that. They did touch each other, express affection. (b—11)

2a. They would do that. (t—1)

b. Yeah. But they wouldn't talk about it with us. We learned it off the street. (b—6)

3a. So you're saying that your parents never sat you down and talked to you about sex. (t—4)

b. You know, I learned it off the street. (b—7)

4a. OK, we'll talk about that. That's another question — What did you learn about sex off the street? — What about nudity? (t—6)

b. That was nothing, like — ah, you know . . . (b—12)

5a. That was sort of natural. (t—1)

b. SILENCE (7 seconds) (Larry) (x—7)

c. Are you talking about when we were kids? (b—1)

6a. Or even today, though. It's safer to talk about ten years ago, you know. (t—4)

b. Because — well, what was it? (b—5)

7a. Nudity, talk about sex, and physical affection. (t—7)

b. Yeah, talking about sex, that was — it was there, but it was controlled. (b—6)

8a. Controlled? (t—1)

b. I mean, it was kinda, you know, like — it wasn't like now, you know, when you couldn't even mention anything about sex. It wasn't like that. (b—9)

9a. It wasn't that strict. (t—1)

b. Because my cousin would make jokes and all that. . . . Like I was saying, it was always under control . . . little kids. (b—13)

10a. It was more open. Is that what were you saying? Were you saying there was more freedom to talk about it the older you got? (t—7)

b. No, it's just what we talked about. (b—3)

11a. The kinds of things you talked about. (t—2)

b. Yeah . . . (b—3)

12a. What about affection? (t—1)

b. Yeah. I mean, it's not like I'd see my folks naked on the couch, no. (laughter) (b—9)

13a. Right. So, quickly, one problem I know I have when I think about this question, I can't ever imagine my parents having sex, or whatever. But the thing is, you know, at least the kids — my parents had ten kids, so I know they went to bed together at least ten times, you know. (laughter) You know, but I still have this trouble connecting that — the reality. (t—25)

b. Yeah, I have that trouble, too. I just couldn't — remember I was saying that they showed signs of affection. But . . . children. (Right. OK, Marilyn.) (b—11)

c. In our family, you know, we have something like, we sit down and talk about sex . . . to understand it, the way the oldest ones — (g—12)

14a. You all do this together. (t—1)

b. Yeah, my mother and father and all the rest of us. And just like he said, 'Control'. In a way I understand, because you have to specialize what you mean, you can't use slang, like vulgar language. (Or street language.) Yeah, you can't use that. But you can express, 'What do you mean? What is this?' (g—21)

15a. So there's a time, you're saying, for questions and answers? (t—3)

b. Um-hm. (g—1)

16a. I don't know, you seem to feel good about that. (t—2)

b. In a way, yes, 'cause . . . (Larry) (g—11)

c. That's — something like that I think is good, too, because it makes for more openness amongst members of the family also, in a sense, you know . . . (b—10)

17a. Helps to tie it up. (laughter) (John) (t—1)

b. My parents talked — (Talk louder.) They talked to me about this, you know. They'd discuss about sex and all that. But I feel like — a lot of times I feel uncomfortable talking about sex. I know that . . . takes place. (laughter) (b—23)

18a. You're saying they're willing to talk to you, though. (t—2)

b. Right. (b—1)

c. See, and in my case, what they're telling me, I know something that they don't know. Because they have . . . and you look at them seriously and all that . . . And I want to get their attention. 'Cause if I try to correct her, she doesn't believe me. (b—20)

19a. She won't listen. (t—1)

b. Right. So I feel, I get angry with her, you know. (b—5)

20a. So, even though she's willing to talk about it, it still sounds strained, right? (Jackie) (t—4)

b. . . . talk about sex . . . (Among yourselves.) . . . You know what I mean? (Name) (g—25)

c. In my family situation, . . . (b—10)

21a. Like you were saying, you learn a lot from your older brothers and sisters. (Alvin, are you agreeing? OK, Shawn.) (t—4)

b. One thing I don't understand, you know, like in my family, even though my mother — I know my father is different — but my mother and my sister are all real close, you know. I mean, talking about sex is nothing in my house — (g—17)

22a. Pardon me, Shawn. (MESSENGER INTERRUPTION) OK, I'm sorry for that, Shawn. Hey, let's settle down. I'm sorry for that interruption. (t—19)

b. That's OK. I don't understand why . . . talk about. My mother talked about it like talking about going to a dance or something. (Like the weather.) It's no big deal. (Right) I mean, I can remember she telling me about sex when I was about eight years old. (g—16)

23a. How did you react as an eight-year-old? (t—2)

b. I think I was curious, you know. (g—3)

24a. Did you ask her? (t—1)

b. I think I used to ask her questions. And my mother, she says, 'Look —' she said, she rather for me to ask her than ask somebody off the street. Because she said, now if I come home pregnant, she said, 'I told you so.' I mean — (laughter) (g—12)

c. My mother — it's no big deal. I'll go home and talk about it tonight, you know. (g—5)

25a. You talk with her about the class? (t—1)

b. Oh, yeah, all the time. (g—2)

26a. What did she say? (t—1)

b. She didn't say nothing. She just say, 'Oh, yeah?' (laughter) (Sharee) (g—3)

c. Like, in my house there's not too much talk about it. Like, if you bring it up, you know, like my father, he'll go back into the . . . You know, and stuff like that. He'd never bring it up. When they did bring it up to me, I didn't hardly know about it, so I just sat there and listened. (laughter) (g—26)

27a. So you're saying that your dad goes off on these tangents, talking — what? — telling stories, or — (t—7)

b. Yeah, or . . . (g—11)

28a. OK, so you're saying they're not so willing to listen or hear your story (t—3)

b. Well, my mother, she like, she's sort of open, she realizes that she can't go back . . . everything. So she's real different from my father . . . (Shawn) (g—17)

c. It's just like sort of — (Speak up.) Just like, sort of like Shawn . . . When I was young, . . . hospital, OK? . . . So I was pregnant, OK? . . . They told me, 'To get circumcised.' And I said, 'What's circumsized?' (laughter) You know, I was real, awful young, you know? . . . She said, 'OK, sit down,' so we talked about it, you know? . . . We talk about it . . . We don't have no certain time. (g—66)

29a. It's not a traumatic event. (t—1)

  b. It becomes a little bit lighter, that's what I want to say. (g—3)

30a. Let's go on to the last topic.

MR W's DISCUSSION — parent–child relations

1a. I don't think they're totally incompatible, the things you're saying. I just think there are two different ways of looking at them. OK? I mean, I think when you say that you're being led to really kinda make your own way more, I think that's a response to that you really are being influenced by a lot of forces beyond — you have to respond to a lot of things beyond your family, beyond the small society. You know? And I think that's what he was saying, that in the past we tended to be limited in those sorts of situations, whereas now we really do need to go beyond your family to be able to deal with those situations, those influences for growing earlier on, maybe. Does that fit, do you think? OK, good. (Regina) [teacher — 46 seconds]

  b. I don't see what Paul and Steve said as two separate ideas. I think that both of them approve of the way things have happened in the past and the future. And that's why I said that in the past, you know, I think that our generation was led to believe that, well, the teenagers, they were young adults, like. The parents were very strict on them. At that point, I remember my father telling me that people were never allowed to contradict their parents, whatever they say, it was accepted, and you weren't able to ask or even think on your own to see if it fit. And I think that, well, I do think that they had a little bit more respect for not only their elders but their peers, too. You know what I mean? (um-hm) And like today, I feel as though we've made some improvement, but we still like, slip back in a slump because, well now our communication is more open, we are able to question, you know, what our parents say, and disagree with it, and everything like that. I'm not saying that it'll work, but you know we can bring it up, not that we're backed down. And we have — even though we improved it that way, we still, we don't have as much respect as for other people or our friends. So I don't look at it as a separate idea, I thing both of them are, you know, a combination. (g—83)

2a. All right, in a way you're taking it in a different element, you know, I think more kinda personal relationships, . . . for one another. But not in the . . . case, because you're saying that there's more — could I ask you why do you think — I mean, I would presume that you think it is good that there is some more opportunity for young people to really voice their own opinion. Why do you think that's important, or necessary, now? (t—32)

b. I think so because, well, in that way, as being taught something, you understand it. There's a difference in being told to do something, understanding it, and being told to do something and doing it because you're afraid of what might happen if you don't. And I feel as though my parents, they were told to do different things then, certain situations were good for them, because this was their parents talking to them, you know, and they weren't going to defy them. Well, if I have another way of thinking, and my mother or father told me to to do something, I'm going to question them. Even if I end up doing it, or if I don't, I still have the priority to question, to think through it. (g—39)

3a. Good, OK, good. I think that's, you know, a really clear analysis. Do you feel that — do your parents themselves even agree that they think maybe it's better that you be able to really question them at times? (t—16)

b. In my family situation? (g—1)

4a. Well, yeah, our parents in general, if you want. (t—3)

b. It's kinda difficult, because my mother seems to be more of a liberal, I guess you would say, and she goes along with me more and I learn an awful lot from her. But my father — and I can't blame him for it — is like, he can only do what he's been taught. And from his parents I know some things I can't say to him, a lot of things I can't question him on. He's more a 'I said it, you do it.' (g—23)

5a. OK, good. That's a really good illustration there. (Steve) (t—4)

b. I agree with her almost all the way up until the end, where she said it should be partly a responsibility of ours. I think the parent should have — there's not enough respect, is what I was trying to say. I feel it should be back the other way. The other way you don't figure out — you lose respect for the parents, let's see, by — you question them. The other way, if you don't question them, you always have somebody to look up to for one answer. (All right. Anna.) (b—30)

c. . . . But I wasn't arguing with (father). (laughter) . . . And he said, 'No.' And I just wanted to know why, you know, what he thought. And he started yelling at me, like, why am I arguing with him? 'I'm not arguing with you, father, I really want to know why.' . . . (g—50)

6a. How do you mean? (t—1)

b. I was wondering 'why?' . . . It's OK, that's human nature. (g—7)

7a. OK, yeah, I mean I don't think that it necessarily is disrespectful. I think it's probably good. I think some people might be just kinda protective. People do try to get into arguments. But — it's human. But there's sometimes people do this want to egg somebody on, to see how they would answer something. But at the same time I think it's legitimate sometimes to just want to know what they think. But that's not like other people do it, so . . . apparently with her father there are certain limits (Tommy) (t—45)

b. You can have all the respect in the world for your parents, but there's no reason why you shouldn't be able to voice your opinion on what you think is right, if your parents don't agree with you. Or sometimes the only reason for talking like that is you're at the age where you should be able to, like if you don't agree with your parents, ask them why. You're not little kids where you have to snap to do everything that they say. (b—24)

8a. All right, how do you maintain the respect? Steve was — you know, that's another problem. Is there a way to really ask for the reasons and that sort of thing without being disrespectful? And where your parents can really maintain their decision as your parents without having to simply say, 'Well, I said so, that's gotta be the way it is' —? (Do you want to talk about that?) (t—26)

b. You don't really lose no respect for them by questioning them. If they tell you to do something, you could ask them why you want to do it and they'll tell you. But if they still want you to do it, you still gotta do it no matter what. No matter what the reasons, if they tell you to do it, you gotta do it. (b—14)

9a. So in the end, the respect might come from accepting their wisdom, whether you understand it or not, huh? (t—7)

b. My parents will say . . . (b—12)

10a. OK. And yet, you know, as Regina was saying, in the past it did tend to be more like that, that parents were considered kinda total authorities, and I mean, it seemed like it wasn't a completely impossible situation for people to live like that, for long times. And yet for us, it just doesn't seem quite right if you don't have at least the opportunity to hear the reasons why your parents do what they do, or — (t—32)

b. . . . (OK. Chris) (s—4)

c. . . . our family has respect and all that kind of thing. When my parents ask us to do something, like housework, there's no question, because you know housework has to be done. Well, if it does come to questioning why they do things they do, you're free (P.A. BELL). Both my parents, they didn't have, when they were children, they didn't have the strict parents, "you have to do this, that's it." My mother was in the hospital all her life, my father was in an orphanage. They never had the strict parents. So when it came to us, we were just like, they treated us as little people . . . I dunno, there was always respect. And yet whenever we wanted it . . . you know, they like to hear what we didn't understand. (OK, good. Tommy). (g—66)

d. Like, most parents when they say, 'Don't question whatever I say,' I think that's a cop-out, because there could be fault in what they're saying and they don't want you to find fault because they want the human authority. (OK. Regina) (b—17)

e. I think he has a point of view or whatever, but I think, taking from what Chris said, that that shows the point of view that parents are human too. And they relate to situations only from what they have been taught. And the way Chris's parents were brought up, it's easy for them to relate to her and understand her feelings, because it sounds like a situation they were in, they probably, you know, had a lot of care and understanding given to them. And just like — I don't know what his name is — but just like he said, some parents are 'Listen to what I say, and you have to do what I say,' and everything — this is because that's the kind of atmosphere they were brought up when they were children. And if you just keep on harping at your parents, what else they going to do? They've been living like that for — what? — 30–40 some odd years. You can't bring them up all over again. So, like it's a situation you have to bear with. You have to try and deal with it on your own. (g—60)

11a. All right. I think this is really a good illustration of how the family, let's say really shows the differences partly just in historical development.

Subject Index

alternatives to questioning
132–67
  student questions 154–8
  teacher signals 158–61
  teacher silences 161–7
  teacher statements 137–53
answers and answering
  discussion 123–7
  general 13–16, 21, 68–70,
    80–1
  recitation 94–5, 101–8
  see also characteristic
    question-answer; question-
    answer interaction

characteristic question-answer
  discussion 93–7, 125–7
  recitation 67–72
  see also classroom discourse;
    question-answer interaction
classroom circumstances 56–9
classroom discourse 12–17
classroom processes 46–7
classroom transcripts
  discussions 120–2, 182–93
    Mr P 182–5
    Mr S 185–9
    Mr T 120–2
    Mr W 189–3
  recitations 86–9, 176–82
    Mr H 87–9, 176–8
    Ms HT 178–80
    Mr L 181–2
    Socrates 86–7
correlated readings
  discussion questions 171–2
  recitation questions 110–12
  student questions 34–6
  teacher questions 75–7

discussion characteristics 120–7
discussion questions
  characteristics 125–32
  pedagogy 128

evaluation of answers 70–2, 80,
  95–7, 109
evaluation of questions 52–3,
  72–4, 82, 109
examination questions 27–8, 47,
  51–2, 79
examples of alternatives to
  questioning 139–66 *passim*
examples of questioning
  discussion 120–2, 182–93
  recitation 87–8, 96, 100–1,
    176–82
  student 8–9, 32–3, 155–7
see also classroom transcripts

learning to use questions *see*
  practical exercises
lecture questions 46, 50–1, 78
listening to students
  student answers 70–1, 101–3
  student question-answer 106
  student questions 29–30

non-questioning techniques *see*
  alternatives to questioning

pedagogy of discussion questions
  127–71
  ask perplexity questions
    130–2
  prepare questions 127–30
  use alternatives 132–67
  use questions and alternatives
    167–71
pedagogy of recitation questions
  97–110
  based on student questions
    103–10
    evaluation 109
    exchange 105–8
    quiz 108–9
    preparation 103–5
  based on teacher questions
    97–103
    ask nice and slow 100–1

listen to answers 101–3
prepare questions 98–9
pedagogy of student questions
23–33
provide for questions 24–8
sustain asking 30–3
welcome questions 28–30
see also student questions
pedagogy of teacher questions
62–75
pose questions 66–72
prepare questions 64–6
reflect on questions 72–5
see also teacher questions
perplexity questions 18–19, 67,
130–1
practical exercises
discussion questions 173–5
recitation questions 112–15
student questions 36–40
teacher questions 77–82
preparation of questions 64–6,
78, 98–9, 103–5, 127–30
presumptions of questioning 20,
23, 36, 61, 93–4, 131
process of questioning 17–33
answering 21
asking 19–21
learning 21–2
preplexity 18–19
purposes of discussion 167–70
purposes of questioning 55–6,
61, 64–5, 89–92
purposes of recitation 89–92,
109–10

question-answer interaction
13–15, 66–72, 92–7, 105–8
question-answer proposition 7,
21–2, 38, 108, 110
questioning behaviors 59–61
questioning techniques *see*
pedagogy of questions;
alternatives to questioning

reading/studying with questions
27, 38–9, 49
recitation characteristics 86–97
recitation questions
characteristics 92–7
pedagogy 99
research on questioning *see*
correlated readings

Socrates' questions 1, 33–4, 77,
86–7, 110–11, 115
student questions
discussion 154–8
general *see* pedagogy of
student questions
recitation 103–8
study questions 46–9, 51–2, 78

teacher questions
discussion 125–32
general *see* pedagogy of
teacher questions
recitation 93–4, 98–101
teacher signals 158–61
fillers 159–60
pass 160–1
phatics 159
teacher silences 161–7
deliberate silence 162–7
non-deliberate silence 167
teacher statements 137–53
declarative statement 137–42
reflective restatement 142–6
statement of interest 148–9
statement of mind 146–8
student referral 149–50
teacher reddition 150–53

uses of teacher questions 46–53
classroom processes 46–7
evaluation processes 52–3
planning processes 47–52